La Lawng: Michif Peekishkwewin

The Heritage Language of the Canadian Metis
Volume One: Language Practice

Manitoba Metis Federation Michif Language Program
Edited by Lawrence Barkwell

Contributors
Norman Fleury
Rita Flamand
Peter Bakker
Nicole Rosen
Lawrence Barkwell

Copyright © 2004, Peter Bakker, Lawrence Barkwell, Leah Dorion, Rita Flamand, Norman Fleury, Robert Papen, Darren Préfontaine, Nicole Rosen, Lynn Whidden, and the Manitoba Metis Federation.

No part of this work covered by the copyrights hereon may be reproduced or used in any form or by any means - graphic, electronic, or mechanical - without prior written permission of the publisher Pemmican Publications Inc. Any requests for photocopying, recording, taping of information storage and retrieval systems of any part of this book shall be directed in writing to the Canadian Copyright Licensing Agency, 6 Adelaide Street East, Suite 900, Toronto, ON, M5C 1H6

National Library of Canada Cataloguing in Publication Data

La lawng: Michif Peekishkwewin: the heritage language of the Canadian Metis: Manitoba Metis Federation Michif Language Program / edited by Lawrence Barkwell.

Includes bibliographical references and index.
Complete contents: v. 1. Language practice / contributors, Norman Fleury...
    [et al.] – v. 2. Language theory / contributors, Norman Fleury...[et al.]
ISBN 1-894717-22-8 (v. 1). – ISBN 1-894717-28-7 (v. 2)

    I. Michif language—Textbooks for second language learners—English speakers. 2. Métis I. Barkwell, Lawrence J., 1943- II. Fleury, Norman III. Manitoba Metis Federation. Michif Language Program IV. Title

Pemmican Publications Inc.
'Committed to the promotion of Metis Culture and Heritage'
150 Henry Ave., Winnipeg, Manitoba R3B 0J7

Printed and Bound in Canada

The Michif Language Program of the Manitoba Metis Federation is financially supported by the Department of Canadian Heritage, Aboriginal Languages Initiative.

Canada

TABLE OF CONTENTS

Volume One: Language Practice

Introduction   1

1. What is Michif
   By Peter Bakker   5

2. The Writing system and Phonology   9
   By Norman Fleury and Lawrence Barkwell
   Consonant Sounds
   Vowel Sounds
   Word Order in Noun Phrases
   Dipthongs and Liaison Consonants
   Insertions
   Pronouns
   Possessives
   Prepositional Phrases
   Adverbs
   Coordinating Conjunctions

3. Conversational Phrases   13
   By Norman Fleury
   Animals
   Days of the Week
   Greetings
   Meals
   Questions
   Clothes
   In the Kitchen
   Weather

4. Topic Specific Vocabulary   19
   By Norman Fleury
   Animals, Birds and Insects
   The Body
   Clothing
   Colours
   Days of the Week
   Food and Drink
   Kitchen
   Michif Foodways
   Michif Medicines

    Months of the Year
    Numbers
    Relatives
    Seasons
    Taste
    Trees

5. Verbs
    By Norman Fleury   29

6. Michif Language Lessons
    By Rita Flamand   35

7. Dictionary
    By Norman Fleury   47

8. Prayers and Invocations
    By Norman Fleury   61

9. Glossary of Terms   63

10. Recommendations for Best Practices for the
    Development of Michif Language Instruction for Adults
    By Nicole Rosen   67

11. Notes on Contributors   85

La Lawng: Michif Peekishkwewin
The Heritage Language of the Canadian Metis
Volume One
Manitoba Metis Federation
Michif Language Program

Introduction

The purpose of this two volume compendium is to give readers with no knowledge of Michif an introduction to the language. Volume One, "Language Practice", provides an introduction to the Michif language and numerous examples suitable for classroom instruction. All of Volume One is based on the language work done by Michif language experts, Norman Fleury and Rita Flamand. Volume Two, "Language Theory", has disussions of a standardized spelling system, verb construction, Michif storytelling examples and an annotated bibliography of Michif resources.

The Michif language is half Cree (an Algonquian language) and half French (an Indo-European language). It is a combined language, drawing its verbs and associated grammar from Cree and its nouns and associated grammar from Michif-French. The Saulteaux language contributes some verbs, sounds and nouns to the combination. The Michif language is unique in world languages: it is syncretic, in that it is not classified as belonging to a single language family.

The Metis National Council declared Michif to be the official language of the Metis Nation at their Annual General Assembly in Saskatoon, Saskatchewan on July 23, 2000.

Michif Declaration – July 23, 2000

As hpinaen li Bon Jeu/Kischay ka Lakittinat lee Michif ota seu la toyr. Meena ashpinaen li Bon Jeu/Kischay Manitoo ta lawng inan, en Michif chi-itayhtahmak, pi en Michif chi-pimawtichik. Ekoushi li Gouvarnimaw di Michif chi-itwayt, Michif si la lawng di li Nawsyoon.

Whereas the Metis emerged in Canada as a distinct nation with a unique culture; and whereas during the genesis of the Metis Nation, Michif evolved as a distinct language of the Metis Nation; and whereas it is recognized within international law that language is one of the requirements of the establishment or reaffirmation of Nationhood; therefore be it resolved that the Metis National Council recognize and declare Michif as the historical and official language of the Metis Nation.

Our prior publication authored by Norman Fleury, *La Lawng: Michif Peekishkwewin* (Winnipeg: Metis Resource Centre Inc., 2000) was part of an initial Michif language awareness campaign. It gave the reader a brief introduction to the unique language of the Metis people. That project far exceeded our expectations. The booklet is now in its third printing and over 3,000 copies have been distributed.

Over the last two years the Metis Resource Centre has posted Rita Flamand's *Conversational Michif Language Lessons* (with streaming audio) on their website. The site has been receiving as many as 2,000 hits per month since its inception. Rita Flamand's course materials are now available from the Metis Resource Centre in a booklet containing 18 lessons and two CD's of the spoken language. Portions of the first version of her language lessons are included in this text. I should point out that there is no standardized or "correct" way to spell Michif because it is an oral language. Therefore the reader will note that several different spelling systems are used throughout this book.

Some time ago, I discussed the issues of standardized writing systems and a lay-reader's guide to Michif verbs with Peter Bakker. In response he has written on each of these topics for this series. He has also provided overview chapters on the genesis of the language and variant dialects. We wish to applaud Dr. Bakker for his untiring efforts and his willingness to volunteer his time and expertise toward the Metis Nation's efforts at recognition and revitalization of the Michif language.

Over recent years there have been many journal and newsletter articles, which describe the Michif language. This interest has been worldwide. Peter Bakker has supplied us with examples in many languages (German, Portuguese, Czech, and English to name a few). Peter has also posted written and spoken examples of Michif on his own website. Norman Fleury and Peter Bakker have also been featured on national radio in Canada on the Canadian Broadcasting Corporation's program, *C'est La Vie* (June 9, 2000).[1]

In Volume One of the series there are chapters with some examples of grammar and other unique features, then a vocabulary, some Michif lesson formats and a dictionary. Next, we provide examples of Michif prayers. The book starts with an overview of the Michif language prepared by linguist Peter Bakker.

In Volume Two of the series, Nicole Rosen has contributed a chapter on "Stress Assignment in Michif." Peter Bakker then gives an overview and introduction to the hardest part of the Michif language – the verb. He has also provided a good review of the various spelling systems used for the Michif language. He points out the advantages and disadvantages of each system. Also in Volume Two, Robert Papen follows with a chapter which presents his analysis of Michif spelling conventions and proposes a unified Michif writing system.

Volume Two of the collection gives examples of Michif songs, Michif storytelling and concludes with an annotated bibliography and a listing of source material on which one can hear the language being spoken.

Michif has been an exclusively oral language since its inception this creates some problems for text based descriptions and teaching materials. Michif language curriculum development has a number of problems that create obstacles to the teaching of the language.[2]

- Lack of universal spelling,
- Variable pronunciation,
- Lack of an accepted dictionary,
- A variety of regional dialectical differences,
- Limited staff who are Michif language speakers and certified teachers, and
- Lack of accepted language standards.

---

[1] www.cbc.ca/insite/CEST_LA_VIE_MONTREAL/2000/6/9.html
[2] The issue of language instruction barriers for Aboriginal languages is given excellent coverage in Rosemary Christensen, *Ojibwe Language: A Competency Exchange*. Duluth, Minnesota: Ojibwe Mekana Associates, 1991.

The lack of availability of immersion events for students is also a major obstacle to learning and speaking the language. In the face of these considerable barriers one could go to great expense to fashion correct or acceptable Michif (and probably fail), or take a pragmatic solution as suggested by Christensen (1991: 4) for teaching the Ojibway language.

A totally static situation develops if practitioners attempt to solve these differences. We decided to ignore these problems, not because we liked the situation, but because we couldn't solve them in the immediate future and still get on with teaching the language. We elected to concentrate efforts on the easiest way to teach Ojibwe in order to meet our immediate goal, and that of our parents: *that children are able to speak in simple sentences, and have a vocabulary of approximately 400 words.* Ignoring big unsolvable problems caused us to look for the easiest way to read, speak, and spell Ojibwe. We use the phonetic way or how the words sound, of spelling words. When a sounding set of syllables are used as tools toward learning, the words used as examples for Ojibwe sounds are English words.

Michif presents additional problems for a phonetic approach. It is primarily based on two languages which have sounds that are foreign to the English language. It also has phonemes in French not found in Cree and vice versa. At the *2002 International Michif Language Conference* the delegates identified a number of present day challenges to revitalization of Michif:

- lack of Michif language resources in the form of books, CD's, internet sites, videocassettes, games, cartoons, etc.;
- need for Michif curriculum development and standardization;
- lack of knowledge and interest in Michif amongst community leaders;
- little public awareness of the consequences of loss of language;
- innacurate history of the Metis people and the Michif language;
- Metis people's embarrassment of speaking a language that was historically derided as "not real French" or "not real Cree."
- few Michif speakers in urban areas; and
- few Michif speakers amongst youth.

As demonstrated in Peter Bakker's Volume Two chapter on Michif spelling systems it is clear that Michif speakers and the linguists studying Michif have created a variety of writing systems based upon the pragmatic need to begin teaching and learning the language. Linguist Robert Pappen from Université du Québec à Montréal has joined in the efforts toward a standardized spelling system by contributing his suggestions in a chapter for Volume Two. In this volume we have also produced an extensive bibliography of Michif learning materials which should be of assistance to those wishing to work on Michif language development.

The importance of Michif language revitalization cannot be over-estimated. My good friend professor Ann Charter told me of her excitement at being able to read the language she had lost many years ago. She recalled speaking Michif with her Kookum, Justine Parenteau (Boucher), and the fact that as a young girl she used to translate English into Michif for her grandmother. She also spoke of rekindled pride in her Metis heritage and roots.

In conclusion, I want to recognize and thank Rosemarie McPherson, Portfolio holder of the Michif Language Program for Manitoba Metis Federation for kindling my interest in this most unique language, for her efforts in teaching her language to me and for allowing me to participate in these most exciting projects.

Lawrence Barkwell
Winnipeg, Manitoba

What is Michif, and What is Called Michif?
Peter Bakker

The word "Michif" is used for languages spoken by the Métis people, and for the Métis people themselves. However, there are a number of misunderstandings about what constitutes the language Michif. Is Michif one homogeneous language? Is there one Michif language or several? Or is Michif a range of varieties between French one the one side and Cree on the hand, with different degrees of admixture?

Before answering these questions, I will first discuss general practices of naming languages and people and the origin of the word Michif.

Names for languages and people

In naming languages and peoples, the same word is often used for a people and a language. The Crees speak Cree, the French speak French, etc. Also in the case of the Métis this is true. The (French-Amerindian) Métis refer to their *language*, or languages as "Michif," and in their own language also to refer to themselves as Michif *people*. Many Métis also use other words when they talk about their people, for instance "Métis." The word "Michif" has been used in English for quite a while already for the language, and more and more also for the people, the Métis or Michifs. The word "Métis" is the current French word for a person of mixed Amerindian and French descent. But where does the word "Michif" come from?

The origin of the word *Michif*

The word "Michif" is, like Métis, originally a French word, but it is long forgotten in mainstream French, both in Québec and in France. It means the same as "Métis," hence a person of mixed biological descent. In the North American context it always means a person of mixed Amerindian and European, in particular French, ancestry. In the early period in New France (roughly what is now Québec) people of mixed ancestry were called "Mitif." This, and not Métis, is the source of the word "Michif." In the variety of French spoken by the Métis, the <t> before <i> is regularly pronounced as <ch> in <chicken>. So the origin of the form is clear: it is from an older variety of Canadian French, namely "Mitif" pronounced by Métis as "Michif."

Michif: a word for people and language

The word for "people" is often the word for their "language." Germans speak German. However, the Métis/Michif people typically speak different languages in different communities. In Manitoba, one can hear Métis speak of Michif Cree, Michif French, Michif Saulteaux and Michif English. Métis speakers of Saulteaux or English, however, never refer to their language as "Michif." The word "Michif" by itself is used only for two clearly distinct languages, both spoken by Métis people in Canada and the USA.

The first Michif is a distinct variety of French spoken in, among others, Saint Laurent and Saint Ambroise in Manitoba and some communities in Saskatchewan and Alberta. The second Michif is a mixture of French and Cree: the actions (the verbs) are all expressed in Cree in this language, and the objects (the nouns) are all expressed in French. Since (names for) languages and people are nouns, the word Michif is used in both languages for the people and also for the language. The first Michif, the distinct variety of French, formed the French input for the mixed language. It is therefore not surprising that both of these languages are called "Michif," because both use the French noun for their people and their language - which is "Michif."

Which languages do Métis people speak?

Métis people not only speak the mixed language Michif and French Michif, but also Saulteaux (Ojibwe), Swampy Cree, Plains Cree, and Woods Cree. It depends where people grow up which language or combination of languages one may learn in the communities. Nowadays, however, English is the mother tongue of the majority of Métis people. Michif French and mixed Cree-French are traditionally called Michif by the speakers themselves. In recent years the Metis of Northwest Saskatchewan have also called their variety of Cree by the name "Michif." (see below).

Can one and the same name be used for different languages?

The name that people use for themselves and their languages is not necessarily the same as the name used by speakers of neighboring languages. It is not at all uncommon to have different (but often related) languages with the same name. The root of the word "Dutch" is the same as the name their neighbors the Germans use for themselves, "Deutsch," in their own language. Another example: "Romani" is an Indic language spoken in Europe. There are also a number of different languages that have the vocabulary in common with Romani, but not the grammatical system. Some of these mixed languages are also called "Romani," but for linguists they would constitute different languages from the Indic language Romani. In South America, the name Garifuna is used for two unrelated, very different, Amerindian languages and even for a kind of French! "Michif" and "Cree" are both used for two distinct languages.

How many Cree languages are there?

In fact, there are not only several languages called "Michif," but also two languages called Cree. I am not referring to the different dialects of Cree, such as Swampy Cree, Woods Cree, Rocky Cree and Plains Cree. These are all part of the language called Cree: the language spoken by First Nations in many Canadian provinces. There is another one: the mixed Cree-French Michif language is also called "Cree" by its speakers.

If you want to say in Michif "I speak Michif," you can say it in two ways. You can say *beekishkwawn awn **Cris/Cree***, (literally "I speak Cree"), and *beekishkwawn awn **Michif*** (literally "I speak Métis"). In First Nations Cree one would say *"ninêhiyawân"* for "I speak Cree," from the root *nêhiyaw* "Cree person, Indian." Michif and Cree are distinct languages, but the name "Cree" is used for both. In Michif it refers to both the mixed language of the Métis, and also to the language of the First Nations. The First Nations only use it for their kind of Cree. Also the Métis of Northwestern Saskatchewan call their language "Cree" in English, "Cris" in French, and in Cree they say *ninîhiyawân* for "I speak Cree."

Northwestern Saskatchewan: a third Michif?

In Northwestern Saskatchewan, roughly between Green Lake and Buffalo Narrows, the Métis speak a variety of Cree with a modest number of French loans. These French loans mostly refer to items and institutions introduced by the mission and schools. A comparison between the Cree and French parts of their language shows that this language came into being independently of the mixed language Michif. In this region there also appear to be huge individual differences between speakers with regards to how much French they use in their speech. The speakers used to call it Cree, but since the late 1980s some of them also began to call it Michif, adding to the confusion about the question whether Michif is one language or several.

Michif: is there a rainbow of mixtures between French and Cree?

Another question that should be discussed is whether there is a continuous range between Cree and French under the label "Michif," or between the mixed language Michif and the French Michif. In other words, is there a range of varieties, from Cree without French, via Cree with a few French words, via the mixture Michif in the middle, to French with a handful of Cree words in the other extreme? No, this is not the case. There are a number of very discrete varieties. Speakers of the Michif French language never use more than five or so Cree or Saulteaux words. The next language is Michif with all nouns from French and all verbs from Cree. There is nothing in between these two. Separately from those, there is the Cree language with some French nouns in Northwestern Saskatchewan. And finally, there are two variants of Cree without any French spoken by Métis in Northern areas. These latter languages are commonly called Swampy Cree or Rocky Cree. All these languages have their own properties, and both speakers and informed linguists can easily distinguish all of these varieties. Again, there is nothing in between.

Dialects of Michif

Of course, like in any language, there are dialects in Michif. The most distinct Michif dialect of Manitoba is the one spoken in the Duck Bay/Camperville area. They speak the mixed language Michif with some more Cree and Saulteaux words - and with a distinct Saulteaux accent. In some communities more French adverbs or postpositions are used than in others. For the rest, the mixed language is remarkably similar throughout North Dakota, Manitoba and Saskatchewan.

Conclusion

In short, there are a number of distinct languages spoken in Métis communities, not a whole continuum ranging from French to Cree. Two of them are traditionally called Michif: the mixture of Cree and French that is the subject of this book, and the variety of French spoken in a number of Métis communities. Two of them are traditionally called Cree: the First Nations Cree dialects, also spoken in many Métis communities, and the mixed Cree-French mixture. Those languages have the same name, but that does not mean that these are one and the same language.

One can never say that the name that the people themselves give to their language is incorrect. We have to accept these labels that they use themselves, even if the language they speak is different from your language with the same name.

The Writing System and Phonology
Lawrence Barkwell and Norman Fleury

The writing system used here is taken from what was developed by Ida Rose Allard at Turtle Mountain Community College. The phonics system is one which those who read and write English will find most natural. The words are written the way English speakers hear them. This means that English spelling forms the basis, so that the w<u>ee</u> in <u>wee</u>pat and <u>ay</u> in p<u>ay</u>tow sound the same as in English. This avoids having to use the French and Cree phonics systems, but it does create difficulties.

In Michif the sounds of the French derived and Cree derived words, are not the sounds of English. In English, the same letters are often used to represent several different sounds. In this system the letters only represent one unique sound. In written Michif there are no 'silent vowels' as found in English. Michif designates animate and inanimate nouns as in Cree. It usually does not designate a masculine and feminine noun as is done in French.

Consonant Sounds
1. "g" is always the hard, plosive sound, as in the English 'good'.
2. "zh" is pronounced as the final sound in the English 'gara<u>ge</u>' or in the French, 'rou<u>ge</u>,' (roo<u>zh</u>). This is a softer s-like sound like the one in the middle of a<u>z</u>ure, or the consonant of the French <u>j</u>e or <u>j</u>olie.
3. "s" is a strong 's' sound and occurs in the Michif words *pee<u>s</u>tikway*, "come in!" and *pa<u>s</u>pawpi*.
4. "h" following a vowel is always pronounced. This is difficult for speakers of English, since true 'h' sounds do not occur after a vowel in English
5. Michif has some vowels which are pronounced with air escaping from the nose (nasalized). French nasalized vowels are represented by the symbol "n" following the vowel, such as *la ma<u>en</u> (main)* for "hand" and *<u>aen</u> garson*, "a boy". Thus, the sound represented by <u>aen</u> is used to represent the nasalized counterpart to <u>ae</u>. It often occurs following <u>m</u> or <u>n</u> and in French origin words (eg. <u>Aen</u>huk and dim<u>aen</u>, "tomorrow"). True 'n's in French words are marked "nn" as in *fari<u>nn</u>*, "flour". The sounds represented by <u>awn</u> is the nasalized counterpart of <u>aw</u>. It occurs frequently in French origin words such as *av<u>awn</u>* and *t<u>awn</u>*.
6. It is necessary to know how 'y's' work in the middle of words, specifically, whether a <u>y</u> following a vowel is to be read as <u>ay</u> or whether the <u>y</u> is to be read with the following vowel. When <u>ay</u> is followed by a consonant, as in *cha<u>y</u>shkwa*, "I want!" or *wa<u>y</u>zoo*, "bird," there is no problem, it is obviously said as <u>ay</u>. However, in words like *eekwashkoupayin*, the <u>a</u> is short and the <u>y</u> is pronounced with the following vowel, *pa-<u>y</u>in*. Likewise in *awta<u>y</u>oohkayt*, the vowel of the second syllable is a short <u>a</u> followed by <u>yoohkayt</u>. In words like *pa<u>yy</u>ek* and *ataw<u>w</u>ayyen*, a double <u>y</u> is written to clearly indicate that the vowel sound is <u>ay</u>. In summary, a single <u>y</u> between vowels goes with the following vowel; when <u>ay</u>, <u>awy</u> and <u>uy</u> appear before a vowel the <u>y</u> is doubled.
7. The "k" sound in Michif is pronounced with very close to a "g" sound if it is found between vowels.

Vowel Sounds

a   The letter 'a' represents a short vowel sound like the English <u>a</u>bout, <u>a</u>round and <u>a</u>stray.or the sound of the French 'l<u>a</u>'. In Michif this sound is found in the words *ki<u>ya</u>*, *k<u>a</u>* and *k<u>a</u>ywash*. In Michif the 'a' never has a long sound like in the English 'mate'. It is always short or part of the long vowels such as 'aw' or 'ay'.

aw	The long sound <u>aw</u> as in the English 'd<u>aw</u>n' or 'f<u>a</u>ther', in Michif words '*t<u>aw</u>nshi*', "how (are you)," and '*t<u>aw</u>pway*', "really." The sequence 'aw' represents a long vowel sound much like the sound of English 'c<u>aw</u>', 'j<u>aw</u>', 'l<u>aw</u>n', or 'r<u>aw</u>'.
ay	The sound of <u>ay</u> as in the English words 'p<u>ay</u>', 'd<u>ay</u>' or 'm<u>ay</u>', in Michif words *ch<u>ay</u>shkwa*, "wait" and *k<u>ay</u>kwawy*, "what."
ae	The short vowel sound as in the English word 'm<u>a</u>n' or the French word 'm<u>ai</u>n'.
y, awy	The sound of the English 'wh<u>y</u>' and the Michif '*kaykw<u>awy</u>*' ("what").The letters <u>awy</u> represent a long sound, a glide made up of the long vowel <u>aw</u> plus <u>y</u>.
e	The letter '<u>e</u>' sounds like the English 'e' in 'm<u>e</u>t', 'v<u>e</u>t', and 'p<u>e</u>t'. In Michif the sound is found in *w<u>e</u>webizhoo* ("swinging") and *s<u>e</u>t*, "seven" or *enn*, "a".
ee	The sequence 'ee' is the long counterpart of 'i', which is short. It sounds like the vowel of English words like 'b<u>ee</u>t', 's<u>ee</u>', and 'fr<u>ee</u>'. In Michif words, *m<u>ee</u>na* (also"), and *k<u>ee</u>* ("past").
eu	Like the French sound in 'd<u>eu</u>x', for example *soufleu*, "mole".
i	The letter 'i' is used to represent a sound similar to the English short vowell 'i' in 'b<u>i</u>t', 'w<u>i</u>sh' or '<u>i</u>n'. Similar to the 'a' sound, the 'i' in Michif never has the long sound of 'night'. In Michif words, *tawnsh<u>i</u>* ("how"), *l<u>i</u>* ('the'), *ras<u>i</u>nn* (herb or root"), and *w<u>i</u>yas* ("meat").
o	As in the English word 'n<u>o</u>'.
ou	Like the sound in the French 't<u>ou</u>t', in Michif words *kim<u>ou</u>wan* ("it is raining") and *booy<u>ou</u>n* ("I quit"). It is a shorter sound than <u>oo.</u>
oo	Like the long vowel sound in the English 'f<u>oo</u>d', and 'c<u>oo</u>l', in Michif words *<u>oo</u>ta* ("here"), *y<u>oo</u>tin* ("it is windy"), *f<u>oo</u>tr<u>oo</u>* ("mink"), *p<u>oo</u>* ("louse") and *b<u>oo</u>youn* ("I quit").
oe, ueu	The sequence of letters <u>oe</u> is used to represent a sound like the English t<u>oe</u> or J<u>oe</u>. In Michif, *d<u>o</u>kteuer*.
oeu	Like the French sound in 'soeur', and 'beurre'
ow	The sequence '<u>ow</u>' represents a vowel sound similar to the English sound in c<u>ow</u>, h<u>ow</u> or n<u>ow</u>. Found in the Michif words *ki-ya-w<u>ow</u>* ("you guys"), *ga-na-t<u>ow</u>* ("I leave him") and *tah-ka-y<u>ow</u>* ("it is cold").
u	As in 'b<u>u</u>t.' In Michif, *li j<u>u</u>ngle* ("jungle") and *weettam<u>u</u>w* ("tell someone").
uy	The letters <u>uy</u> represent a short glide corresponding to the long glide in <u>awy</u>, e.g. 'g<u>uy</u>', or in Michif *kaykw<u>uy</u>* ("something").
y, awy	Like the English sound, 'wh<u>y</u>'.In the middle of a word it is sometimes difficult to know whether a 'y' following a vowel is to be read as 'ay' or as 'y' with the following consonant. When 'ay' is followed by a consonant there is no problem eg. *Way-zoo* ("bird"). A

single 'y' between vowels goes with the following vowel. In words like *payyek* and *atawwayyen*, a double 'y' is written to clearly indicate that the vowel sound is 'ay'.

Word Order in Noun Phrases

Some French derived adjectives precede nouns; others follow, as in French. Cree based relative clauses can both precede and follow the noun phrase. French based relative clauses can only follow the noun phrase. The noun phrase differs from French in that the numeral precedes the article in Michif and Michif has a different possessive order. Michif possessives have the order: possessor – possessive pronoun – possessed.

Dipthongs and Liaison Consonants

In Michif an [e] or [h] between two consonants is dropped: e.g. chemin becomes *shmen*, cheveaux becomes *zhveu*, Métis becomes *Michif,* petit becomes *pchi* and cheval becomes *zhwal*.

French normally has 'liaison' consonants which are placed between two vowels and which display underlying consonants. For example, the French plural article *les* is normally pronounced [le], but before a vowel-initial noun the underlying 's' shows up, for example, in *les artistes*, "the artists," pronounced *lezartist* in standard French. In Michif this kind of liaison does not exist. In Michif these liaison consonants become part of the noun In Michif a 'z' is often inserted e.g. "Toes"—*lee zartay,* "the number"—*li zounbr* or "trees"—*li zarbre*. This liaison letter seems to have carried over onto the noun even when it stands alone:

French	Michif	English
arbre	*zarbr*	tree
étoile	*zetwel*	star
oeuf	*zoeuf*	egg
os	*zo*	bone
oignons	*zawyoun*	onion

For words with 'di' there is more than a reduction to a dipthong in Michif. The 'd' absorbs the 'i' with the patalization to a resulting 'j'. For example:

French	Michif	English
dix	*jis*	ten
diable	*jiab*	devil
dieu	*Bon Jeu*	God
mardi	*marji*	Tuesday
radis	*rawjee*	radish
dîner	*jinee*	dinner
dimanche	*jimawnsh*	Sunday

Insertions

Cree morphology has a process of 't' insertion between a prefix ending in a vowel and a stem beginning with a vowel. This occurs in both Cree and Michif Cree which may have the following forms:

Ayaw	he has it (inan)	
Ki + ayan	kitayan	you have it (inan)
Apiw	he sits	
Ki + apin	kitapin	you are sitting

Pronouns

I	niya
He/she	wiya (literally, that person)
We	niyanawn, kiyanawn
Me	niya
They/them	wiyawow
Us	kiyanawn, niyanawn

Possessives

Mine	dipayhtaen, niya anima
His/hers	wiya anima, son
Yours	kiyawnow, kiyawow anima
Their	wiyawow

Prepositional Phrases

The majority of prepositional phrases in Michif are derived from French. Two Cree postpositions are used in Michif: <u>ouschi</u> (from, out of, about) and <u>ishi</u> (like, as).

Adverbs

Adverbs in Michif are fairly equally divided between French and Cree derivation. Sometimes both are used.

From Cree	English
mitouni	completely
tapway	very much
mawshkoot	perhaps
kaykawt	hardly (almost)
outa	here
weepat	early
mawka	nevertheless
tuhkinay	always

From French	English
dimaen	tomorrow
bon matin	early
la	presently
toul tawn	always
kawnmaem	nevertheless
tad baen	perhaps

Coordinating Conjunctions

Coordinating conjunctions may also be either Cree or French.

From Cree		From French	
akwa	and	pi	and
meena	and	i (et)	and
mawka	but	me (mais)	but
keeshpin	if	si	but

Conversational Phrases
Norman Fleury

Animals
I saw a moose.
Aen nariyael geewawpamow.

That is a dog.
Aen sh'yaen ana.

I see a gray kitten.
Aen pchi minoosh gree niwawpamow.

I like fish.
Li pwasoon nimiyaymow.

He killed four ducks.
Katr kanawr kee nipahayw.

Days of the Week
Today is Monday.
Laenjee anoush.

Tomorrow is Thursday.
Zhweejee dimaen.

Yesterday was Sunday.
Iyayr Jimawnsh.

We will meet on Friday.
Vaundarjee ka nakishkawtanan.

There are seven days in a week.
Il y a set zhour den smenn.

We are going to work all day Saturday.
Ka atoushkanan tout la zhournee Samjee.

Greetings and Niceties
Hello.	Tawnshi
How are you?	Tawnshi kiya?
How are you? (plural)	Tawnshi kiyawow?
I am fine.	Nimiyou ayawn.
What is your name?	Tawnshi eyishinikawshoyan?

My name is…	Dishinikawshon…
How's the weather?	Tawnshi ayshikeeshikawk?
Still the same.	Ekoushi kiyawpit.
How about you?	Kiya mawka?
I'm the same, too.	Ekoushi neeshta.
For sure.	Tapway outi.
How are they?	Tawnshi wiyawow?
How do you feel?	Tawnshi itamaschihouyen?
Where are you from?	Tawnday pe'oototayan?
I'll see you again.	Meena ka wawpamitin.
Thank you for coming.	Marsi, eki pe'itootayan.
Where did you go?	Tawnday kaw itoustayyen?
Come and visit sometime.	Paykeewkay ahpee.
What did you say?	Kaykwawy kaw itwayyen?
What are these?	Kaykwawy oonhin?
What is this?	Ooma?
What would you like to do?	Kaykwawy ay noostay oushistawyin?
Can you do it?	Kashkistawn cheen?
Yes. You too.	Wee. Keeshtawow.
I don't understand.	No nishtoohen.

Meals

Kaykwawy kaw meechiyen?
What did you eat?

Kay kwawykaw minihkwayyen?
What did you drink?

Ni nohtay awpawkwawn.
I'm thirsty.

Kaykwawy nohtay minehkwayyen?
What do you want to drink?

Wetoushpahminan.
Eat with us.

Nimoya gee meetshoun anoush.
I haven't eaten today.

Ga minihkwawn. (Noohteh minihkwawn.)
I'd like a drink.

Keenoohtaykatawn chee?
Are you hungry?

Dan li café nu meetshoonan.
We are going to eat at the restaurant.

Li tea ga minihkwawn.
I'll have some tea.

Li boulet di Michif weehkatishahahk.
The Michif meatballs are delicious.

En pouchinn gee-oushihow pour li Zhoor di Lawn.
I made bag pudding for New Years.

Tou li zhour li rababoo geemeechinawn.
We ate rababoo every day.

Li kawfee kishitayw.
The coffee is hot

Lee pataek tahkeshowak.
The potatoes are cold.

Woosham ni geeshpoun eyanah chee meetshooyan.
I'm too full to eat any more.

Kahkiyuw nu doo meetshoonan awndor law oma.
We are all going out to eat now.

Questions

Tawnshi kiya?
How are you?

Kiya mawka?
How about you?

Tawnday weekichik?
Where do they live?

Awanaw awa?
Who is this?

Awanaw kiya?
Who is it?

Tawnshi eh itwayk awn Michif?
How do you say it in Michif?

Tawnshi eh itaytamawn?
What do you think?

Tawnda eh itohtayen?
Where are you going?

Si kwarik chee ooma?
Is this O.K?

Ki wapamow chee anoush?
Did you see him/her today?

Tawnima ikouhketakihtayk?
How much does it cost.

Tawnshi eh shinikawshooyen?
What's your name?

Keenoohtaykatawn chee?
Are you hungry?

Kaykwawy ooma eh shinikawtek?
What's this called?

Tawnshi kiyawow?
How are all of you?

Tawnshi wiya?
How is he/she?

Tawnshi ta famee?
How is your family?

Tawnshi wiyawow?
How are they?

Ti paree? (cheen)
Are you ready?

Clothes

En shmeezh neu ayow.
He has a new shirt.

Tahkoupita tee kwardoon.
Tie your shoe laces.

Kaychikoo pi kawshimoh.
Undress and go to bed.

Tawnday mon kapo d'hiver? (parka)
Where is my parka?

Taenehkhay ikouhk li bitaen kaw atawwayt?
Why does he buy so many clothes?

In the Kitchen

Ouyeshtawshou.
Set the table.

Kakisheepayyawkanew.
He will wash the dishes.

Kakisheeppayyawkanewak.
They will wash the dishes.

Li fournoo kishitayw.
The oven is hot.

Kawmanishwew lee cake?
He/she will cut the cake?

Weather

Ga wawchin.
I feel cold.

Its chilly.
Tahkawyow.

Mishpoun.
It's snowing.

Iyary kee kishitayw
Yesterday was quite warm.

Kimouwan.
It's raining.

Ka mishpoun dimaen.

Hippopotamus	aen hippoo
Kitten	aen pchi minoosh
Koala bear	aen noor sheenwayn
Lion	aen lyoon
Llama	aen groo mwatoun
Lizard	aen lezawr
Louse	aen poo
Mare	enn zhoumaw
Marten	aen martinn
Mink	aen foutroo
Mole	aen soufleu
Moose	aen nariyanl
Mosquito	aen maraeñgwaen
Otter	enn loot
Owl	aen yeeboo
Ox	aen beu
Parrot	aen parachay
Peacock	aen peacock
Penguin	aen paengwaen
Pheasant	aen fezawn
Pig	aen kwashon
Polar bear	noor blawn
Rat	aen raw'd grawnzh
Raven	aen koorboo
Rabbit	aen lyayv
Rhinoceros	aen animael si kom aen kwashoon (aen rhinoo)
Rooster	aen kouk
Shark	aen groo pwesoon d'mayr
Sheep	aen mwatoon
Skunk	aen shikawk
Snake	enn koulayv
Sow	enn trweey
Squirrel	enn swiss
Steer	aen zhen beu
Tit(bird)	aen nwayzoo
Toad	aen krapoo
Turkey hen	enn daend
Turkey tom	aen gwadaend
Turtle	aen torcheu
Weasel	enn blet
Wolf	aen loo
Wolverine	weehtikouhkawn

The Body

Arm	li braw
Armpit	disour le braw
Back	li doo
Behind, (buttocks)	daryayr
Belly	vawntr

Blood	li sawn
Body	li kor
Bone	aen zoo
Brain	la sarvel
Breast	l'istamaw, gee-gee
Brow	sousis
Calf of leg	awn aryayr ta zhawnb
Cheek	la zhoo
Chin	li mawtoon
Elbow	li koudr
Eye	zyeu
Eyebrows	lee sousis
Eyes	lee zeux
Face	li vizaezh
Finger	aen dway
Fingernail	enn zoung
Foot	aen pyee
Forehead	li fron
Hair	lee zhveu
Hand	la maen
Head	la tet, kishtikwawn
Heart	li choer
Heel	aen taloun
Hip	la hawnsh
Index finger	li dway ou bur lipous
Kidney	aen royoon
Kidneys	lee royoon
Knee	aen zhnoo
Knuckles	lee zhwaencheur
Lash	aen fwet
Leg	enn zhawnb
Lip	babinn
Liver	oushkawn, li jeur
Lower arm	awn baw ton braw
Lower leg	awn baw ta zhawnb
Lung	pwamoo
Molar	enn grous dawn
Mouth	la boush, la yol, ki-toon
Neck	li koo
Nose	li nee, kichawn
Nostril	enn nawrinn, aen trou'd nee
Nostrils	lee trou'd nee, lee nawrinn
Shoulder	li poul, nipoul
Skin	la poo
Sole of foot	disour lee pee
Stomach	li vawntr
Teeth	lee dawn
Thigh	la fess
Thumb	li pous (poos)
Toe	aen nartay, aen zartay
Tongue	la lawng

Tooth	enn dawn
Upper arm	awn laer ton braw

Clothing

Apron	aen tableeyee
Beads	lee rasaed
Belt	enn saencheur
Bonnet	aen bwanaen
Boot	lee groo souyee
Button	aen bwatoon
Cap	enn kasket, aen peacap
Clothes	li bitaen
Clothing	li bitaen
Coat	aen kapoo
Diapers	enn koush, braye
Dress	enn rob
Earring	pawn daray
Earrings	lee pawn daray
Glove(s)	aen gawn, lee gawn
Hat	aen shapoo
High heel	lee grawn taloun
Jacket	aen zhilay
Moccasin	souyee moo
Nylons	lee baw d'sway
Overcoat	aen kapoo, aen grawn kapoo
Pants	enn kilot
Parka	aen kapishoon
Rag	enn gineey
Ribbon (hair)	roubawn di zhveu
Ring	aen zhoon
Sash	saencheur fleshay
Scarf, shawl	aen shawl, enn krimon
Scarf	enn krimonn
Shirt	enn shmeezh
Shoe	aen souyee
Shoes	lee souyee
Skirt	enn rob di faem
Slipper	lee shaosur
Socks	lee baw
Stockings	lee grawn baw
Sweater	aen sweater
Trousers	la kilot
Underwear	li bitaen ditsoor
Winter hat	aen shapoo d'ivayr

Colours

Black	nwayr
Blue	bleu
Brown	shakwalaw
Gold	l'or

Gray	gree
Green	vayr
Orange	orawnzh
Pink	kouleur di rooz
Purple	vyalet nwaenr
Purplish	nawachikoo vyalet
Red	roozh
Silver	larzhawn
Vermillion	varmiyoon
Violet	vyalet
White	blawn
Yellow	zhounn
Yellowish	nawutchikou zhounn

Days of the Week

Sunday	Jimawnsh
Monday	Laenjee
Tuesday	Morjee
Wednesday	Mikarjee
Thursday	Zhweejee
Friday	Vaundarjee
Saturday	Samjee

Food and Drink

Apple	enn pom
Bacon	lawr boukanee, or li bacon
Banana	enn banann
Bannock	la galet
Bean	enn fayv, lee beans
Beer	la byayr
Beets	lee betraev
Berry	enn grenn
Bread	li paen, puhkwayshikun
Bread (fried)	lee bengnyee (also donut)
Butter	li bueur
Cabbage	la shoo
Cake	aen kayk, cake, aen gatoo
Carrot	enn karot
Catfish	la barbeu
Cheese	li framazh
Cherry	lee mireez
Chicken meat	la vyawnd di poul
Coffee	li coffee
Cottage cheese	dilet coutt
Cream	la krem
Cucumber	lee kokoom
Curd	dilet sur (seur)
Drinks	lee drink, (hard liquor) la bwesoon
Egg	aen zaef
Eggs	lee zaef

Fish	li pweson
Flour	la farinn
Food	li mawnzhee
French bean	lee fayv kanayaen
Fruit	li fruit
Grape	enn grep
Grapes	lee grep
Ham	li zhawnboon
Herb	enn rasinn
Honey	li myel, li honey
Horseradish	enn ragee di zhwal
Ice cream	l'ice cream or la krem a glaes
Jackfish	li brochet
Juice	li zheu or li joose, juice
Lard	li saendou, la gres
Lemon	aen sitron
Lemonade	li lemonade or li drink di sitron
Liquor	la bwaysoon
Meat pie	tart di vyawnd
Meat	la vyawnd
Meat ball	lee boulet
Melon	aen melon
Milk	dilet
Mirabelle (plum)	enn prenn
Mushrooms	lee mushroom
Mustard	la moutard
Noodle	li makaroonee, ka kinwowk
Nut	enn pakawnn
Nuts	lee pakawn
Oats	la wen
Oil (vegetable)	li wil
Onion	lee zayoon
Orange	aen narawnzh
Pancakes	lee krep
Paprika	li pwayvr roozh
Pasta	li mawnzhee di makaroonee
Pea	aen pwaw
Peas	lee pwaw
Pemmican	li tooroo
Pepper (vegetable)	lee pwayvr di zhardaen
Pepper (herb)	lee rasinn di pwayvr
Pickerel	li doray
Pie	la taert
Pinto bean	li feyv kawy
Poppy	lee poppy
Porridge	li porij
Potato(es)	enn patak, lee pataek
Prune	lee prenn
Pudding	la pouchinn
Pumpkin	enn sitrooy, aen pomkinn
Radish	rahjee

Raisin	lee razaen
Raspberries	lee frawmbwayz
Rhubarb	la roubarb
Rice	li ree
Roll	li pchee paen
Rolls	lee pchee paen
Salad	la salad
Salt	li sel
Sausage	soosis
Sorrel	bloon (colour)
Soup	la soup
Spinach	li spinach
Strawberry	enn frayz
Strawberries	lee frayz
Sugar	li seuk
Tea	li tea, li tee
Toast	lee tous, en toast
Tomato	enn tomat
Tomatoes	lee tomat
Trout	la trut
Vegetables	lee zhardinaezh
Vinegar	li vinaegr
Water	diloo
Wheat	li blee
Wine	li vaen

Kitchen

Bowl	enn bowl, bol
Butter dish	li buerueyee
Chair	enn shayzh, ita chi-ashpapihk
Dishes	la visel
Fork	enn fourshet
Knife	aen koutoo
Oven	aen fournoo
Pepper shaker	li pwayvryee
Plates	lee zassyet
Spoon	enn chouyayr
Stove	aen pwel a chweezin
Sugar bowl	li seukriyee
Table	la tab
Toothpicks	li bois di dawn

Michif Foodways

Bannock bread	la galet
Black haws	lee za leez
Buffalo esophagus	feuyet de buffalo[3]
Chokecherries[4]	la grabdour, lee tukwahiminawna

---

[3] The *feuyet* is the internal part of the buffalo's esophagus used to make an indescribably delicious Michif soup.
[4] Chokecherry syrup with *la galet* was a common dish.

Gooseberries	lee groozel
High bush cranberries	lee pabinaw[5]
Juneberries	lee pwayr
Meatballs	li boulet
Pemmican	li tooroo
Pinchberries	lee mireez
Pudding[6]	la pouchinn
Rose hips	lee bon toond rouzh
Stew[7]	li rababoo
Thorn apples	lee snel
Tripe dish	la pawns or li dibree

Michif Medicines

French	Michif	English
La racine noir	la rasinn nwyar (kaskate-ocepihk)	black root " "
Belle angelique	bel anzhelik	flagroot, sweet flag, or red flag
Li boum	li boum	wild mint
Le baume de champs	li pawpermen, li pchi boum	wild mint, wild peppermint
Le baume sauvage	li boum savaezh	wild mint
Le tabac	li tabaw	tobacco (ceremonial)
La roche rouge	la rosh di peup	red pipestone[8]
L'herbe du saint	l'arb a saent	wild sage[9]
Herbe de saint Jean	l'arb di saent Jean	ginger
Le pied de coq	l'arb a daend	turkey weed[10]
?	akandamus	water lily
La médicine sucré	la michinn seukree	sweet Anne's, sweet anise
?	li rasinn moonahashkwek	seneca root, snake root
?	maskigus	swamp root
	li kounouy	cattail
Plantain	lee plantain	plantain, frog leaf
Gingembre	sayzhawn	ginger
La hars rouge	la harrouzh Kinnikinnik	Red Willow

Months of the Year

January	Zhawnvyee
February	Fevriyee
March	Mawr

---

[5] The Metis settlement of Pembina gets its name from the high bush cranberry.
[6] Also called *son-of-a-bitch-in-a-sack*.
[7] Made with rabbit, chicken or sage hen.
[8] Red pipestone was grated into a powder and either taken one teaspoon dry followed by water or mixed with water then taken. This was a remedy for boils and skin infections.
[9] Boiled as a tea and taken for colds, fevers, intestinal flu and pinworms.
[10] The blossom which looks like a cock's foot is used for backache and kidney diseases.

April	Awvree
May	Mee
June	Jwaen
July	Jouyet
August	Ahou
September	Septawmbr
October	Oktobr
November	Novawmbr
December	Disawmbr

Numbers

Hen (Payyek)	One
Deu	Two
Trwaw	Three
Kaet	Four
Saenk	Five
Sis	Six
Set	Seven
Wit	Eight
Naef	Nine
Jis	Ten
Oonz, hoonz	Eleven
Dooz	Twelve
Trayz	Thirteen
Katorz	Fourteen
Kaenz	Fifteen
Sayz	Sixteen
Ji set	Seventeen
Jiswit	Eighteen
Jiznef	Nineteen
Vaen	Twenty
Trawnt	Thirty
Karawnt	Forty
Saenkant	Fifty
Swesawnt	Sixty
Swesawnti jis	Seventy
Katravaen	Eighty
Katravaen jis	Ninety
San	Hundred
Mil	Thousand
Milyoon	Million

Relatives

Although most nouns in Michif are from the French, the nouns for relatives in Michif are from both French and Plains Cree.

Ni mawmaw, ma mayr	My mother
Ni pawpaw, mon payr	My father
Mon frayr	My brother
Ma soeur	My sister

Ni moushoom — My grandfather
Ki moushoominawn — Our grandfather

Nookoum — My grandmother
Kookoum — Your grandmother
Oohkouma — Her grandmother
Oohkoumiwawa — Their grandmother

Nooshishim — My grandchild
Nooshishimak — My grandchildren
Mon nook — My uncle
Ma tawnt — My aunt

Mon kouzaen — My cousin (m)
Ma kouzinn — My cousin (f)
Ma yaens — My niece
Mon niveu — My nephew
Leu niveu — Their nephew

Dittawawak — In-laws by marriage

Seasons
Summer — l'etee
Fall — l'atom, takwawkwun
Winter — ivayr
Wintertime — awn n'ivayr
Spring — li praentawn
Springtime — kaw-see-kwahk

Taste
Its bitter — mawyishpakwun
Its sour — sheewow
Its sweet — weeskashin

Trees
Ash — li frenn
Aspen — li trawnb
Birch — li bouloo
Burdock — grachias
Cottonwood — li l'yawr
Elm — loerm
Oak — li shenn
Pine — li pinet
Red willow — la hawroozh, kinnikinnik
Tree — aen arbr
Willow — li soul

Verbs
Norman Fleury

Ask	kwaychihkaymou
Bathe	kisheepaykee
Believe	tawpwayhtamihk
Blow	pootawchikay
Chase (to)	na washwayhk
Chew	mawmawkwaschikayhk
Climb	awmachiwayhk
Comb (to)	sheekahouhk
Come	paytouhtayw
Come (all)!	awshtamik!
Count	akisschikay
Cry (to)	mawtouhk
Cut (to)	manishamihk
Detour	wawshakahtay
Dish up	kapatayhikay
Divide	tawshkina
Drag (to)	pimitawpayhk
Dressed (get)	pousstashawkawn
Drink	minihkwayhk
Drive	paminkayhk
Eat	meechishouhk
Forget	waneehkayhk
Get off	neetakoushee
Get up (to)	pashikoohk
Go home	keeway
Go on	niyawn
Hang on	kikamou
Hurry (all)	kakwayyawhouhk
Jump	kwawshkwahtay
Kiss (to)	ouchayhkayhk
Laugh (to)	pawhpihk
Leave	shipwayhtay
Look	kanwawpahta
Losing	wanihtawniwan
Lost	wanishik
Move	mawshee
Pull it	ouchipita
Read	amischikay
Ride	pooshi
Run	pimbastaw
Say	itwayhk
Say (to)	chee itwayhk
See (to)	chi wawpahtamihk
Set, place	ashtaw
Sing	nakamou
Sleep	nipaw
Sorry	mitawtamihk

She/he heard it.	Kee payhtum.
She/he heard you.	(Ki) kee paytawk.
He/she heard me.	Gee paytawk.
You heard me.	Kee payhtawin.
I heard you.	Kee paystatin.

To be Ill

I am ill	Dawkoushin
You are ill	Ki awhkoushin
He/she is ill	Awhkoushiw
We (not you) are ill	Dawhkoushinawn
We (all of us) are ill	Ki awhkoushinawn
You (plural) are ill	Ki awhkoushinawwow
They are ill	Awhkoushiwak

To Wait

Wait for him/her.	Payhih.
Are you still waiting?	Keeyawpit cheen ki payhoon.
Let's wait for him/her.	Payhawtawk.

What are we waiting for?
Kaykwawy ay payhtawyahk?

What are you waiting for?
Kaykwawy ay payhtawyen?

Transitive verb forms:

To see

I see him/her	Ni wawpamow
You see him/her	Ki wapamow
She/he sees her/him	Wawpamayw
You see me	Ki wawpamin
I see you	Ki wapamitin
He/she sees you	Ki wawpamik
He/she sees me	Ni wawpamik

To search

I am searching for him/her	Ni natounawow
You are searching for her/him	Ki natounawow
She/he is searching for him/her	Natounawayw
You are searching for me	Ki natounawin
I am searching for you	Ki natounawitin
He/she is searching for you	Ki natounawik
He/she is searching for me	Ni natounawik

To hear

I heard him/her	Gee paystawow
You heard him/her	Kikee paystawow

He/she heard him/her	Paystawayw
You heard me	Kikee paystawin
I heard you	Kikee paystawitin
She/he heard you	Kikee paystawik
He/she heard me	Gee paystawik

The transitive verb form changes when the object is inanimate, as follows:

I see it	Ni wawpastaen
You see it	Ki wawpastaen
He/she sees it	Wawpastum
I am searching for it	Ni natounaen
You are searching for it	Ki natounaen
She/he is searching for it	Natounum
I heard it	Gee paystaen
You heard it	Kikee paystaen
She/he heard it	Kee paystum

She/he has a pig and a dog.

Root verbs with prefixes, suffixes, past tenses:

1.   Piihtikwew.   She/he is coming in.
   prefix - **pe**   **Pe**piihtikwew He/she came in.
   suffix - **ag**(k)   **Pe**piihtikwew**ak** They came in.

2.   Wewbizhoo.   She/he is swinging.
   Prefix - **wii**   **Wii**wewebizhoo. She/he will swing.
   Suffix - **ag**   Wewebizhoo**ak**. They swung.

3.   Maadoo.   She/he is crying.
   Prefix - **wii**   **Wii**maadoo. She/he will crying.
   Suffix - **wag**   Maadoo**wak**. They were crying.

4.   Yoodin. It is windy.
   Prefix - **wii**   **Wii**yoodin. It is going to get windy.
   Past tense - **kii**   **Kii**yoodin. It was windy.

4.   Kanawe'itam.   She/he keeps it.
   Prefix - **wii**   **Wii**kanawe'itam. She/he is going to keep it.
   Past tense - **kii**   **Kii**kanawe'itam. She/he kept it.

Nouns: Plural and Singular:

1.   Tomaat tomato
   plural - lii   lii tomaat, the tomatoes
   singular - li   li tomaat, the tomato
   singular - aen   aen tomaat, a tomato

2.   Zaayoñ   onion
   plural - lii   lii zaayoñ, the onions
   singular - li   li zaayoñ, the onion
   singular - aen   aen zaayoñ, an onion

3.   Shapoo/bonne   hat
   plural - lii   lii shapoo/bonne, the hats
   singular - li   li shapoo/bonne, the hat
   singular - aen   aen shapoo/bonne, a hat

4.   Kateñ   doll
   plural - lii   lii kateñ, the dolls
   singular - li   li kateñ, the doll
   singular - aen   aen kateñ, a doll

5.   Kwaashoñ   pig
   plural - lii   lii kwaashoñ, the pigs
   singular - li   li kwaashoñ, the pig
   singular - aen   aen kwaashoñ, a pig

Lesson 2

Relatives:

My mother	Ni maamaa
My father	Ni paapaa
My brother	Mon freyr
My sister	Ma suer
My grandfather	Ni mooshoom
Our/your grandfather	Ki mooshoominaan
My grandmother	Nookum/kookum
Our grandmother	Nookuminaan/kookuminaan
Your (plural) grandmother	Kookumiwaw
His/her grandmother	Ookumaa
Their grandmother	Ookumiiwawa
My grandchild	Nooshishim
My grandchildren	Nooshishimaak
My uncle	Mon nook
My aunt	Ma tawnt
My cousin (male)	Mon koozeñ
My cousin (female)	Ma koozin

Michif Conversation:

Ni maamaa kiishishew la galet.
My mother is baking bannock.

Ni paapaa kahkiiyaw kii moowew.
My father ate it all.

Mon freyr pi ma suer kii moowewak kookum/nookum sa galet.
My brother and my sister ate grandmas bannock.

Ni mooshoom kii nikootew li bwaa.
My grandfaqther chopped wood.

Ookumaa kii li soupiike'iwa.
Her grandmother made supper.

Zhaweimaawak/zhaagiaawas nooshishimak.
I love my grandchildren.

Mon nook pi ma tawnt zhaweimigonaanik.
My uncle and my aunt love us.

Ndo shooshkotawaanan avik mi kooz'inaanig.
We go skating with my cousins.

Ni mooshoominaan nihtaa niimiw la jig.
Our grandfather is a good stepdancer.

Kookumiiwaw waakoomew nookuma.
Your grandmother is related to my grandma.

Ookumiiwawa kii petaa'iwa la michin.
Their grandmother brought medicine.

Lesson 3

Outdoor conditions:

Kimiwan.
Its raining.

Niishkaatan/machi kiishigaw.
The weather is bad.

Kishinaw.
Its cold.

Taake'ayaw.
Its chilly.

Mishpoon.
Its snowing.

Toneur.
Thunder.
Lii chiiraañ
Northern lights.

Kizhitew
Its hot (weather).

Miiyoukiishikaw.
It's a nice day.

La grel.
Hail.

Ikwaashkwan.
Its cloudy.

Shiikwan.
Spring.

Niipin.
Summer.

Takwaagan
Fall.

Pipon.
Winter.

Aabawaw.
Mild weather.

Numbers 11 to 20:

Ooñz	eleven	Saeñz	sixteen
Dooz	twelve	Jis set	seventeen
Trayz	thirteen	Jis wit	eighteen
Katorz	fourteen	Jis naef	nineteen
Kaeñz	fifteen	Vaeñ	twenty

Michif Conversation:

Pe piitikwaahik lii deu shen, wii kishinaw daahor.
Bring the two dogs in, its going to get cold outside.

Wii itoohtew dañ ligliiz Jimaash.
He/she is going to church on Sunday.

Wiipach wii niipin ekwa ta kizhitew.
It will be summer soon and it will get hot.

Kii mooshoominaan kii peshoowew treez lii zhvoo egwa peyaak aen zhwal kii nipoo.
Our grandfather bought thirteen horses and one of the horses died.

Niwii ndo niiminaan Samjii ooswer.
We are going dancing on Saturday night.

Ki kiiwaapahten chiiñ lii chiiraañ Vanderjii ooswer?
Did you see the northern lights on Friday night?

Lesson 4

Review of Sentences:

Taanishi kiya?
How are you?

Taanishi eyishinikaashoyan?
What is your name?

Taande pe'itoohteyan?
Where are you from?

Pe piihtikwe yoodin daahor.
Come in, its windy outside.

Kakiiyaw lii zaañfañ wewebishoowak.
All the children are swinging.

Ni mooshoom kii nikootew li bwaa.
My grandfather chopped wood.

Zhawe'imaawak/zhaakiaawak nooshishimak.
I love my grandchildren.

Wiihtootew dañ ligliiz Jimaash.
He/she is going to church on Sunday.

Niwii ndo niiminaan Samjii ooswer.
We are going dancing on Saturday night.

Ki kiiwaapahten chiiñ lii chiiraañ Vanderjii ooswer?
Did you see the northern lights on Friday night?

Michif Conversation:

Poohkchishkam en shapoo oshtikwaanihk.
He wears a hat on his head.

Wiishaage'itam si daañ.
She has sore teeth.

Apishaashina tii pii/kitaapishishiidaan.
You have small feet.

Aahkoshew sa vaantr.
She is sick to her stomach.

Miiyoushiniiyew sa boosh/miiyoutoonew.

She has a lovely mouth.

Son nii aapishaashiniiyew
He has a small nose.

Kii shaakinam sa laañg.
She stuck out her tongue.

Wiishake'itaam sii zhaañb, sii zhnoo, sii talooñ pi son pii.
He has sore legs, knees, heel and foot.

Noya mooshitaw sii zartey.
He does not feel his toes.

Lesson 5

Numbers 30 to 100:

Thirty	traant	Seventy	swisaanti jis
Fourty	karañt	Eighty	katreevaen
Fifty	saenkaañt	Ninety	katravaen jis
Sixty	swisaañt	Hundred	sawn

Michif Conversation:

Mitooni ki miiyoushken ta shmiizh.
Your shirt fits you well.

Taapwesa ko miyoushken toñ saeñcheur fleshey.
Your sash really looks good on you.

Toñ kapishoñ poochishka, machi kishinaw.
Wear your parka, it's getting cold.

Poochishka tii sooyiimoo avik tii klak.
Wear your moccasins with your moccasin rubbers.

Poochishka toñ saenchur avik ta kilot.
Wear your belt with your pants.

Taanehki ekaa wechi/ochi poochishkawachik tii gaawin pi toñ krimonn avik toñ kapot?
Why don't you wear your gloves and scarf with your coat?

Poochishkaawik tii baaw avik tii sooyii.
Wear your socks with your shoes.

Lesson 6

What, When, Where, How, and Why:

What - Kekwiy

Kekwiy ooma?	What is this?
Kekwiy aanima?	What is that?
Kekwiy nemaa?	What is that over there?
Kekwiy oñihi?	What are these?
Kekwiy ozhitaayan?	What are you doing?
Kekwiy ka meetshouyon?	What did you eat?
Kekwiy ka miniikweyan?	What did you drink?
Kekwiy pe naataman?	What are you coming for?

When - Taanishpii

Taanishpii wii pekiiwiikeyan?
When are you (singular) coming to visir?

Taanishpii wii pekiiwiikeyek?
When are you (all) coming to visit?

Ishpii kiiweyani.
When I go home.

Ishpii kiiwechi.
When he/she goes home.

Ishpii waapamachi.
When you see him/her.

Ishpii waapamaaki.
When I see him/her.

Ishpii waapamaachi.
When I see him/her.

Where - Taande

Taande lii klii?
Where are the keys?

Taande tii kriyooñ?
Where are your pencils?

Taande kaa itoohteyan?
Where did you go?

Taande kaa itoohteyan?
Where is he going?

Taande pe ootohteyaan?
Where are you coming from?

Taaniiwaa?
Where is he/she?

How - Taanishi

Taanishi kiya?
How are you?

Taanishi wiiyaawaw?
How are they?

Taanishi e'izhitaayan ooma?
How do you do this?

Taanishi e'itaamachihoyan?
How do you feel?

Taanishi ka e'ishi wiishaakishik?
How did he/she get hurt?

Taanishi e'ishi kishke'itak?
How does he know?

Kiya maaka? Kikaashkitaan chiiñ?
How about you? Can you do it?

Why - Taanehki

Taaneki wechi maadooyan?
Why are you crying?

Taaneki kaa ochi kishiwaashiiyan?
Why did you get angry?

Taaneki kaa ochi miiyishk?
Why did he/she give it to you?

Taaneki ekaa ochi piikishkwet?
Why isn't he talking?

Taaneki ekaa ochi poochishkak aen bone?
Why won't she wear a hat?

Michif Conversation:

Taanishpii wii pe kiwikeyan?
When are you coming for a visit?

Sipaa, wipach etookwen.
I don't know, soon I guess.

Taande kaa itooteyaan Samjii ooswer?
Where did you go on Saturday night?

Gii ndo niimin.
I went dancing.

Taanishi e'itaamachihoyan?
How do you feel?

Nimiyoumaachihoon ekwaa.
I am feeling fine now.

Kekwiy wii ozhitaayan kiiweeyani?
What will you do when you get home?

Nka kishiipekinen ma visel.
I'll wash my dishes.

Taanehki wechi kashke'itaaman?
Why are you sad?

Akoz ni mooshoom ekii nipoonyit soñ zhwal.
Because my grandfather's horse died.

Lesson 7

Opposites:

inside / outside	walk / run
di daawñ / daahor	pimoohte / pimipaahtaa
white / black	bald / hairy
blaañ / nwayr	tikwawnayw / plaen'd zhveu
high / low	go / stop
ishpaawaan / baañ	niiyaañ / nakii
cold / hot	smells good / stinks
kishinaw / kizhitew	miiyoumaakwan / wiichekan
get in / get out	sharp / dull
piihtikway / wayawee outa	kiinow / ashaastin
stand / sit	come / go
niipaa / api	aashtam / shipwehte
put on / take off	Heaven / Hell

puchishka / kechikona

push in / pull out
aakinaki / chipitaa

young / old
zhenn / viyeu

same / different
la mem/parey //paahkaan

I like / dislike
Ni miiyayiten / bakwaaten

Today / tomorrow
anootch / dimaeñ

frozen / thaw
aakwaatin / tihkitayw

fix / break
oushtaw / piikoona

wife / husband
ma faam / mon vyeu

up / down
aañ leuraañ / baañ

big / small
gro / pitchi

hard / soft
mushkaywow / youshkow

tall / short
kinooshiw / chakooshew

li syel / lañ fr

God / Devil
Li bon Jeu / li jiyaab

before / after
avañ / apre

ahead / behind
di vaañd / aryear

alive / dead
pimaatishew / nipoo

ugly / beautiful
maayaatishiw / katawaashis

angry / glad
kishiiwaashew / miiye'itam

begin / stop
maachitaa / pooyoow

wet / dry
shaapopew / paashtayw

clean / dirty
peehkun / viinan

open / shut
pawshtaynaa / kipaha

cry / laugh
maatoo / paahpi

man / woman
aen nom / eñ faam

Michif Conversation:

Ka waapamitin chiin dimaeñ?
Can I see you tomorrow?

Ndo chomishin dimaeñ, la simen ki vieñ maaka?
I am very busy tomorrow, how about the coming week?

Kitaa awiiyashoomitin chiiñ ti sooyii apre dimaeñ?
Can I borrow your shoes, day after tomorrow?

Announcer	l'annooseur	**B**	
Annually	tout lee zawn		
Answer	nashkoum	Baby	aen pchi beebee (bay bee)
Ant	enn frimee, enikoons		
Anteater	li frimee kaw moow awt	Babyhood	Tawnd pchee
		Back (body)	li doo
Antelope	lee kabree	Backbone	li taenchee
Antique	kawyawsh kaykwuy	Backward	nashpawchipayin
Ape	aen groo shaenzh	Backwoods	li grawn bwaw
Appetite	enn bonn apichee	Bacon	lawr boukanee or li bacon
Apple	enn pom		
Apple	enn pomm	Bad	vilen
Appreciate	kishcheetayistum	Badger	aen brayroo
April	awvree	Bag	aen sawk
April	li mwawd Awvree	Baking oven	aen fournoo
Apron	aen tableeyee	Bald	pashkoushtikwawnayw
Apron	aen tableeyee	Ball	enn plot
Argue	nashchinawsyoon	Banana	enn banann
Arm (lower)	awn baw ton braw	Bandage	wawaykinikiun
Arm (upper)	awn l'aer ton braw	Bank (financial)	la bawnk
Arm	li braw	Banner	aen poviyoun
Armchair	enn grous sayz (shayzh)	Bannock (bread)	la galet, puhkwayshi-kun
Armpit	disour le braw		
Armpit	disour li braw	Banns	lee bawnd maryaezh
Aroma	miyoumawkwuhk	Baptism	lee batem
Arrow	enn flesh	Barbed wire	la brosh a pawr
Arrowhead	tet di flesh	Barbeque	rouchee
As	kowm	Barber	aen barbyee
Ash (tree)	li frenn	Bare	emoushtayawhk
Ash Wednesday	li Zhoor dee Sawndr	Bareback	pat sel
Ash	li frenn	Barefoot	pat souyee
Ashes	la sawndr	Bareheaded	pat bwanaen
Ashtray	enn ashtray, enn sawndreyee	Barely	akawwawt
		Barenaked	pat bitaen
Ask him/her	kwaychim	Bargain	bon marshee
Ask me	kwaychimin	Bark (dogs)	mikiw
Ask them	kwaychimik	Bark (tree)	li kors
Ask	kwaychihkaymou	Barley	lorzh
Aspen	li trawnb	Barn owl	lee yeeboo di taeb
Aster	enn fleur zhoun	Barn	aen nitaeb, taeb
Atop	awnd seu	Barrel	aen kawr
Attach	shakamoutawhk	Barrow	enn barwet
Attic	la shawmbr ishpimihk (awn layr)	Basement	la kaev
		Bashful	neepaywishiw
Auburn	roozh shakwalaw	Basin	laev maen
Auction	aen nawkawn	Basket	aen payeen
August	ahou	Bassinet	li baybee soon payeen
August	Awawnd Awhoo	Bat	aen shouri shoud
Aunt	ma tawnt	Bath	pakawshimou, keesheepaykeen
Autumn	Latonn		
Award	aen pree	Bathe	geesheepaykeen
Awl	aen nalen	Bathroom	enn shawmbr ita chi pakawshimook
Axe	enn hawsh		
Axle grease	li gwadroun	Battery	enn batree
Axle	aen nisyeu	Bead	enn rasaed
Azure	bleu blem		

Beads	lee rasaed	Billygoat	li mawl di shevr
Beadwork	la garnicheur	Birch	li bouloo
Bean	enn fayv, lee beens	Bird	aen nwayzoo
Bear	aen noor	Birth certificate	bawtistayr
Bearskin	la pou'd door	Birth	nihtawwawkiw
Beatle	aen manichoose	Birthday	tipishkum
Beautiful	katawashishiw	Biscuit	aen biskwee
Beaver	aen kastor	Bishop	li Vek
Because	akooz	Bison	li bufloo
Become	kee-ishpayiw	Bit (bridle)	li mor di brid
Bed	aen lee	Bitch	la shyenn
Bedbug	enn pinayz	Bite	enn boushee
Bedding	lee drawd lee	Bitter	mawyishpakwun
Bedsore	pakoushiniw	Bittern	li bitor
Bee	aen yawmoo	Black and blue	nwayr pi bleu
Beef	li baef	Black bear	aen noor nwayr
Beehive	enn nik di yawmoo	Blackfoot	lee Pyee Nwaenr
Beer	la byayr	Black haw	leezaleez
Beets	lee betraev	Black measles	la rouzhol nwayr
Before	avawn	Black oak	li shenn nwayr
Begin	mawchi	Black pepper	li pwayvr nwayr
Behind (buttocks)	daryayr	Black spruce	li pinet nwayr
Behind	awn aryayr	Black	nwayr
Belch	paykatay	Blackbird	aen nitournoo
Believe	tawpwaysta	Blackfoot	lee Pyee Nwayr
Bell	enn klosh	Blackout	gee wanikishkishin
Belly button	li noobree	Blacksmith	aen forzhoun
Belly	li vawntr	Blacksnake	enn koulayv nwayr
Bellyache	gishoshkatawn	Blackstrap	la milaes nwayr
Belt	enn saencheur	Blanket	enn kouvart
Bench	li bawn	Blaze	awn flamb
Bend down	nawakee	Blazer	aen zhilay
Bend	pihkina	Bleach	wawpawshtayw
Beneath	awnt sour	Bleed (nose)	gipishtanawn
Benediction	la binidiksyoon	Bless	li bineew
Bequeath	nakatamawkayhk	Blind man's bluff	ou ka li mayaw
Berry picking	moowoushouk, mooshoo	Blind	namoo wawpiw
		Blinder	lee gardizyeu
Berry	enn grenn	Blindfold	geekipwawpahpitikwuk kipwawkipish
Beside	akoutee		
Best man	li promyee garsoon d'oneur	Blinding	gipwawpahoukoun
		Blink	pashahkwawpiw
Best	miyoer	Blister	aen boufeed doo
Bet	ushchikayw	Blizzard	peewun, enn poudiree
Better	nawut miyou-awshin, pleu boon	Blond	aen bloon
		Blood	li sawn
Beware	payhtuk, manaw	Blood sausage	li boudin
Beyond	kwawshchipayin	Bloody	plaend sawn
Bib	enn bavett	Blow	pootawchikay
Bible	la bib	Blue	bleu
Bicker	keehkawstowawk – nawatastouwuk	Boar	aen vayraw
		Board	enn plawnsh
Big	mishow, groo	Boast	mamishchimouhk
Bile	li fyel	Boat	aen bawtoo
Bill	aen bek	Body	li kor
Billiards	ou boul	Boggy	yooshkow

Boil	ousha, kaw oushamihk
Bone	aen zoo
Bonnet	aen bwanaen
Boogieman	aen Kookoosh
Book	aen leevr
Boot	lee groo souyee
Born	nihtawoukihk
Bottle	enn beutay or la boutay
Bow legged	wawkikawtayw
Bow	aen nark
Bowel	la grous trip
Bowl	enn bawl
Box	enn bwet
Boy	aen garsoon
Boyfriend	kwvalyee
Braid	lee kwet
Brain	la sarvel
Branch	enn brawnsh
Brave	braev
Bread (fried)	lee baenyee (also donut)
Bread	li paen
Bread pudding	la pouchinn di paen
Break	peekouna
Breakfast	li dezhawnee
Breast	l'istamaw, gee-gee
Brick	enn brick
Bricks	lee brick
Bride	la zhen maryee
Bridesmaids	lee fee doneur
Bridge	aen poon
Bridle	enn brid
Bring	paytaw
Brook	enn pchit koolee
Broom	aen balay
Brother (older)	nishtesh or mon teh teh (for a special older brother or sister)
Brother	mon frayr
Brow	sousis
Brown	shakwalaw
Brush	enn brush
Bucket	enn shayayr
Buffalo	li bufloo
Bug	manichoosh
Bull	aen tooroo
Burdock	grachias
Burn	mayschisha
Bury	nahinayw
Butter dish	(li) beuriyee
Butter	li beur
Butterfly	aen memaengwaen
Buttermilk	dilet di beur
Button	aen bwatoon
Buy	atawway
By	araw

C

Cabbage	la show, la shoo
Cabin	enn kabann
Café	li café, aen restorawn
Cake	aen kayk, cake, aen gatoo
Calendar	aen kalawndreyee
Calf of leg	awn aryayr ta zhawnb
Calf	aen voo, pchi voo
Call	taypway
Camel	aen shamoo
Camera	aen kararaw
Candle	enn shawndel
Candy	lee kawndee
Canoe	aen kanoo
Cap	aen bwanaen aen peekap
Car	enn shawr, aen awtamoobil
Cariboo	aen kariboo
Carpenter	aen nouvriyee
Carpet	aen tapee
Carrot	enn karott
Casket	aen sorkay
Cast iron	la foond
Cat	aen minoush (pousis, sha)
Catechism	li katshim
Caterpillar	aen groo vayr pweleu
Catfish	la barbeu
Cattail	lee kounouy
Cattle	lee zanimoo
Cattle or buffalo stomach	la pawns
Ceiling	li plawfoon
Cellar	enn kaev
Certain	sartaen
Chair	enn shayzh, ita chi-ashpapihk
Chase (to)	washwayhk
Cheek	la zhoo
Cheese	li framazh
Cheetah	aen groo shat (pousis, minoush)
Cherry	lee mireez
Chest (body)	l'istamaw
Chest (furniture)	enn valeez
Chew	mawmawkwashikayhk
Chicken meat	la vyawnd di poul
Chicken pox	la pikot
Chicken	enn poul
Chicks	lee (pchi) poulay
Chilly	tahkayow
Chin	li mawtoon
Chokecherry	takwahiminawnaw
Church	aen Igleez, L'igleez

Claw	enn grif	Dark	tipishkow
Claws	lee grif	Day	enn zhournee
Clean	payhkun	Dead	nipoow, mor
Clear skies	wawshayshkwan	Deaf	kaypishayw, aen soor
Climb	awmachiway	December	disawmbr
Cloth	li laenzh	Deep	timeew
Clothes	li bitaen	Deer	aen shouvreu
Clothing	li bitaen	Delicate (tender)	wawhkaywishiw
Cloud	enn nwawzh	Detour	wawshakahtay
Cloudy	yeekwashkwun	Devil	jiab, or jyab
Coal	li shawrboon	Diapers	enn kush, braye
Coat	aen kapoo	Different	puhkawn
Cock	aen kok	Digging seneca root	moonahashkwehk
Coffee	li coffee	Dinner	jinee
Cold (object)	fret or tahkawwa	Dish up	kapatayhikay
Cold (weather)	kishinow	Dish	la visel
Collostrum cake	li flawn	Dish water	loo'd visel
Colours	lee kouloer	Dishes	la visel
Colt	aen poulaan	Divide	tawshkina
Comb (to)	sheekahouhk	Doctor	li dokteur
Comb	aen paeny (noun), sheekahouken (verb)	Dog	li sh'yaen
		Dogwood bark	hart roozh, (The Michifs used this as a tobacco substitute.)
Come (everybody)	awshtamik		
Come here	ashtum oota		
Coming	payyawwak	Doll	enn kataen
Communion	La Komeeyoon	Dolphin	aen groo pwesoon di mayr
Corn	bladaen		
Cottage cheese	dilet digoutee	Domineering	nahayhtawishiw
Cottonwood	li l'yawr	Don't	kawya
Count	akischikay	Donkey	aen milait
Country	payyee	Door	la port
Cousin	mon kouzaen (m), ma kouzinn (f)	Dough	la pawt
		Drag (to)	pimitawpayhk
		Dress (noun)	enn rob
Cow	enn vash	Dressed (get)	poustashawkawn
Cracklings	lee gortoon	Dried meat	kwkkehwauk, la vyawnd shesh
Crawl	pimitawchinoow		
Crazy	keeshkwayw, (foo)		
Cream	la krem	Drink	minikkway
Creator	creatoeur	Drinking glass	aen ver kawminihkwawkayhk
Cree	lee Cree		
Cricket	aen krichay (aen manichoosh)	Drinks	lee drink, (hard liquor) la bwesoon
Crow	enn kwarnay (kornai)	Drive	paminikay
Cry (to)	mawtouhk	Drizzle	awun
Cry	aen mawtout	Drop	patinamik
Cuckoo	aen koukoo	Drops of brandy	la dawns di kroshay (the dance)
Cucumber	lee kokoom		
Cup	enn bol	Drown	kawnishtawpawwayhk
Curd	d'let sur (seur)	Drug	la michin
Curtain	li ridoo	Duck	aen kanawr
Cushion	la koushinn	Dumplings	lee grawdpayr
Cut (to)	manishamihk	Dust	la pousyayr
		Dye	atisha

D

Dance	kawneemihk enn dawns

E

Each	shakaen, shaek
Eagle	l'aegl, aen groo nway-zoo
Ear	aen zaray, aen naray
Early	weepat
Earring	pawn daray
Earrings	lee pawn daray
Earth	la tayr
Easter	Li Zhoor di Pawk
Eat	meetshou, mawnzh
Edge	ou bor, ou bout
Egg	aen zaf
Eggs	lee zaf
Eight	wit
Elbow	li koudr
Elephant	aen elefawn
Eleven	hounz, oonz
Elk	la bish
Elm	loerm
Embarrass	neepaywishik
Ember	aen cheezoon, enn brayz
Embrace	awmbraes
Empty	sheekwow, aryaen di-dawn
End	akoushi, li bout
English	Awnglay
Enough	akoushi, asee, nawnsee
Enter	peehtikway
Equal	paray
Erase	kawsheepayha
Error	pacheehkay
Escape	kicheew, tapasheew
Especially	sourtoo
Eventually	peeyish
Ever	weehkawt
Everywhere	mishiway itay
Exchange	mayshkoutouna
Exert	sheeshcheehishouhk
Expel	waywaypinayw
Eye	zyeu
Eyebrows	lee sousis
Eyes	lee zheu, zyeu

F

Face	li vizaezh
Fade	wawpawshtayw
Fainted	wanikishkishiw
Falcon	enn sort di mawnzheur di koulayv
Family	la famee
Farmer	aen farmyee
Fat	li graw
Father	pawpaw
Fawn	aen pchi shouvreu
Fea	enn peus
Feather	enn plem
February	fevriyee
Female	enn fimel
Fence	aen pawr
Fever	la fyayv
Fiddle	aen vyeloon
Field corn	bladaend
Field mouse	aen sooree
Field	aen shawn
Fifty	saenkant
Fight	noutinikay
Filet	pawnishikayk
Filter	sheehkoupawtina
Fin	enn zel di pwesoon
Finch	aen pchi twayzoo
Find	mishka
Finger (index)	li dway ou bur lipous
Finger	aen dway
Fingernail	enn zoung
Finish	pooyou
Finished (I'm)	boh-yoon
Fire	aen feu, shashkitayw (verb)
First	pramee
Fish	li pwasoon
Fisherman	lee pwasoon kaw pakatawawchik
Fishhook	aen napesoon
Fist	pwaen
Five	saenk
Fix	oushtaw
Flag	aen paviyoon
Flat footed	napakishitayw
Float	pimawtakow
Floor	li plawnshee
Flour	la farinn
Fly	enn moush
Fog	la brem
Folk dance	enndawns di Michif
Food	li mawnzhee
Foot	aen pyee
Forefathers	nimoushoomipan
Forehead	li fron
Forever	nawshpichi, pour tout boon
Forget	waneehkayhk
Fork	enn fourshet
Four	kaet
Fox	aen rnawr
Fragile (tender)	wawhkaywishiw
Freeze	awhkwatin
French bean	lee fayv kanayaen
Friday	vawndarjee
Fried bannock	lee beng

Fright	shaykishiw
Frog	enn gournouy
From	oushchi
From	oushi
Fruit	li fruit
Fry	shawsha, shawshishikayk
Full	plaen
Funeral	l'awntayrmawn
Furnace	la or enn fournaenz
Furry	pweleu

G

Gale	mishiyoutin
Gall stone	enn rosh di fyel
Gambler	aen gambleur
Game	aen zheu
Garden	aen zhardaen
Gate	enn bawryayr
Get along	miyouweechayhtouk
Get away	tapashee, pashpee
Get off	neetakoushee
Get up (to)	pashikoohk
Get	nawta, vatawn
Gift	aen presawn
Giraffe	aen giraffe
Girl	enn feey
Girlfriend	enn jaeng, ma bloond
Glad	miyeustamihk
Glass	enn vitr
Glove	aen gawn
Glove(s)	aen gawn, lee gawn
Glue	la kol
Go home	keeway
Go on	niyawn
God	Li Boon Jeu
Godfather	aen pawrawn
Godmother	enn mawrenn
Gold	l'or
Gone	ashpin
Good Friday	Vawndarzee Saen
Good	si bon
Goose	aen zway
Gooseberries	lee groo zel
Grab	outihtina
Grain	li graen
Grandfather	ni moushoom
Grandmother	nouhkoom
Grape	enn grep
Grapes	lee grep
Grass	li fwaen
Grasshopper	enn soutrel
Grave	enn fous (noun)
Gray	gree
Gray squirrel	enn swiss gree
Green	vayr
Grief	weeshakitayhayw
Gun	aen feezee
Gunpowder	la poudr a feezee

H

Hail	la grel
Hair	lee zhveu
Half hour	enn dimiyoer
Half	la mochee, la mwachee
Halter	aen likoo
Ham	li zhawnboon
Hammer	aen martoo
Hand	la maen
Hang on	kikamou
Happy	koontawn, miyeustaen
Hare	aen lyayv (wawpoos)
Hat	aen shapoo
Haul	awataw
Have	ayow
Hay	li fwaen
He/she	wiya (literally, that person)
Head	la tet, kishtikwawn
Head cheese	la tet di framawnz
Heal	keekayhk
Health	la sawntee
Hear	payhta
Heart	li choer, keur
Heat	kishitayw
Heel	aen taloun
Hello	tawnshi
Help me	weechihin!
Help	weechihiway
Hen	enn poul
Her (him, she, he)	wiya
Herb	enn rasinn
Here	oota
High heel	lee grawn talour
Hill	enn kot, enn beut (knoll)
Hip	la hawnsh
Hippopotamus	aen hipoo
His/hers	wiya anima, son
History	tawn'd kayawsh
Hit	pakama
Hole	aen troo
Home	neekinawhk
Honey	li myel, li honey
Hood	kapishoon
Horse – colt	aen poulaen
Horse – filly	enn poulish
Horse – gelding	aen zhwal
Horse – mare	enn zhoumaw
Horse – stud	aen etalloon

Nut	enn pakan
Nuts (crazy)	keeshkwayw
Nylons	lee baw d'sway

O

Oak	enn shenn
Oats	la wenn
Obey (obedient)	natouhta
Obstinate	shasheepistam
Ocean	lamayr
October	oktobr
Odor	miyawkwun
Off	kaychikouna
Oil (vegetable)	li wil
Oilcloth	li tapyee'd taeb
Oily	toumow, graysee
Old, old man	aen vyeu
Once in awhile	awshkuw
One hundred	san
One	henn or payyek
Ongoing	toul tawn
Onion	lee zayoon
Only	pikou, mouschi
Or	abaendoon, ou baen
Orange	aen narawnzh
Organ	aen norgann
Orphan	keewaetish, aen arfalaen
Other	lee zootr
Otter	enn l'oot
Outside	dahor, awnd hor
Oven	aen fournoo
Overcoat	aen kapoo, aen grawn kapoo
Owl	aen yeeboo
Ox	aen beu

P

Pacer (horse)	aen nawnbleur
Painful	weeshakayistawkwun
Paint	la paenchur
Pair	enn payr
Pale	blem
Pan	aen plaw
Pancakes	lee krep
Pants	lee kilot
Paprika	li pwayvr roozh
Parka	aen kapoo d'iver, aen kapishoon
Parrot	aen parachay
Pass away	nipoow
Passage, corridor	ita shipimoostayhk, aen pawsawzh
Pasta	li mawnzhee di makaroonee

Pea	aen pwaw
Peacemakers	la pay ka oushtachik
Peacock	aen peacock
Peas	lee pwaw
Peel	pooshakin
Pelt	lapoo
Pemmican	li tooroo
Pen	enn pleum
Pencil	aen kriyoon
Penguin	aen paengwaen
People	li mood
Pepper (vegetable)	lee pwayvr di zhardaen
Pepper shaker	li pwayvreyee
Pepper (herb)	li pwayvr
Perplexed	awn pen
Pheasant	aen fezawn
Pickerel	li doray
Picture	aen partray
Pie	la tawrt
Pig	aen kwashoon
Pigeon	aen peezhoon
Pill	enn pileunn
Pincherry	li mireez
Pine (tree)	li pinet
Pinto bean	li fayv kawy
Pipe	enn peup
Pistol	aen pistalay
Pitcher	aen pot a let
Pitchfork	enn foorsh a fwaen
Plate	aen nasyet
Plates	lee zasyet
Polar bear	aen noor blawn
Policeman	enn polis
Poor	poovr
Poppy	lee poppy
Porcupine	aen portipik
Pork	di lawr
Pork hocks	lee pat di kwashoon
Porknpuffs (cracklings)	lee gorton
Porridge	li porij
Pot	aen pot, enn shayayr
Potato	enn patak
Potato(es)	enn patak, lee pataek
Potato soup	la soup di patak
Powder	la powdr
Prairie chicken	aen faezawn'd prayree
Pray	amihaw
Prayer beads	aen shaplay
Prune	lee prenn
Pudding	la pouchinn
Pull back	ouchipuyhoow
Pull it	ouchipita
Pull out	kichipita
Pull	ouchipita, manipishik, weekoow

Pumpkin	enn sitrooy, aen pom-kinn	Right now	shaymahk
Purple	vyalet nwaenr	Right, true	tawpway
Purplish	nawachikoo vyalet	Ring	aen zhoon
		Road	shmaen
		Roast	rouchee

Q

Quadrille	la ril a kaet
Quart	enn kwart
Queen	la renn
Quit	pooyoo, nakata (leave it alone), nakeek (stop)

R

Rabbit	aen lyayv
Rabbit soup	la rababoo di lyayv
Raccoon	aen shaw savaezh
Racehorse	aen kooreur
Rad bird	li ptsi twayzoo roozh
Radish	enn rajee
Rag	enn gineey, aen laenzh
Railroad	li shmaenn'd fayr
Rain	la pwee (noun), payshtow (verb)
Raisin	lee razaen
Rake	aen rawtoo
Raspberries	lee frawnbwayz
Rat	aen raw'd grawnzh
Rattlesnake	aen sarpawn sonet
Raven	aen koorboo
Razor	aen rawzway
Read	amischikay
Ready	paree
Recall	gishkishin
Red oak	li shenn roozh
Red River Cart	en shawret
Red River Jig	Oayâche Mannin
Red River	La Rivyar Roozh
Red willow	la hawroozh, kinikinik
Red	roozh
Reel of Eight	la Ril a Wit (dance)
Reel of four	la Ril a Kaet (dance)
Relation	la parawntee
Remind	kishkishoum
Rent	li rent
Rhinoceros	aen animael si kom aen kwashoon, (aen rhinoo)
Rhubarb	la roubarb
Rib	aen plakootee
Ribbon (hair)	roubawn di zhveu
Rice	li ree
Rice pudding	la pouchinn di ree
Rice soup	la soup di ree
Rich	rish
Rid	waypina, waypin
Ride	pooshi

Robin	rouge gorzh, griv
Rock	enn rosh
Roll	li pchee paen
Rolls	lee pchee paen
Room	enn shawmbr
Rooster	aen kok
Roots	la rasinn
Rosin	larkawnsyoon
Rot	pooree, panawtann
Rough	rof, papikwow
Round	roon
Row(line)	aen rawn
Rubbers	lee klak
Rug	aen tapee
Run away	tapashee
Run	pimbastaw

S

Sack	aen sawk
Saddle	enn sel
Saint	aen saen
Salad	la salad
Salt	li sel
Sand flea	enn peus di sawbl
Sash	saencheur flechee
Saskatoons	lee pwayr
Saturday	samjee
Saucer	aen niskoup
Sausage	soosis
Sawhorse	aen zhwulay
Say (to)	chee itwayw
Say	itwayhk
Scarf	enn krimonn
Scissors	li seezoo
Sea shells	leekwacheey
See it (to)	chi wawpahtamihk
Set, place	ashtaw
Seven 1	set
Shaking Hand Day	Shakishchenetewin (New Years Day)
Shark	aen groo pwesoon d'mayr
Shave	kawshkipawashouwuk, peestousha
Shawl	aen shawl
She	wiya, en fimel
Sheep	aen mwatoon
Shelf	enn kornish
Shirt	enn shmeezh
Shoe	aen souyee

Shoes	lee souyee		would be "he who shoots the arrow."
Shoulder	li poul, n'ipoul		
Sing	nakamou	Stove (kitchen)	aen pwel a chweezinn
Soiux (people)	lee Sioux	Straight	dret, mitoumi
Sister	ma soeur	Strawberries	lee frayz
Sister (younger)	nisheemish	Strawberry	enn frayz
Siter (older)	nimish	Student	aen zhawn d'ikol
Sit! (command)	apik!	Sugar bowl	li seukriyee
Six	sis	Sugar	li seuk
Skin	la poo	Summer	l'etee
Skirt	enn rob di faem	Sun	li salay
Skunk	aen shikawk	Sunday	jimawnsh
Skunk glands	la mus di shikawk	Sweater	aen sweater
Sled	enn trenn	Sweep	waypahikay
Sleep	nipaw	Swim	pakawshimouhk
Slipper	lee shauseur	Syrup	li seeroo
Small	pchee, pchi		
Snake	enn koulayv	**T**	
Snow geese	li zway blawn	T.V.	li T.V.
Snow	la neezh	Table	(la) tab
Socks	lee baw	Tail	la cheu
Sole of foot	ton awm	Talk with	kitoutayw, kitoutitin
Sorrel	bloon (colour)	Talk	peekishkway
Sorry	mitawtamihk	Tank	la tank
Soup	la soup	Tea dance	l'apray mijee kawneemihk
Sour cream	la krem seur		
Sour milk	dilet kawyee	Tea	li tea, li tee
Sow	enn trweey	Tease	nawachihiway
Spinach	li spinach	Teeth	lee dawn
Spoon	enn chouyayr	Telephone	aen foonn
Spring	li praentawn	Tell	weehta
Square dance	aen square dance, enn kwadril	Ten	jis
		Tender (soft)	wawhkaywishiw
Squirrel	enn swiss	Tent	tawnt
Stable	li taeb	Testify	timwaenyeen
Staircase	aen niskalyee	Thank you	marsee, or marsee kititin, sometimes megwetch from Saulteaux or ki nas koumitin from Cree are used as well. For "I thank you" use ki naskoumitin
Star	aen zetwel		
Starting new tanawn	awn neu ni mawchis-		
Steer	aen zhen beu		
Steps	aen paw, lee paw, lee marsh diskalyee		
Stew	li rababoo	That	ana (animate) eg. Enn patak ana (That is a potato).
Still	kiyawpit		
Sting	cheeshoow		
Stink	weeshaykun	That	anima (inanimate) eg. Enn shezh anima. (That is a chair).
Stockings	lee grawn baw		
Stomach	li vawntr		
Stop	nakee, pooyoow (quit)	Thaw	tihkitayw
Storm	enn tawnpet	The	la, li, lee
Stormy	machikeeshikow	Their	wiyawow
Story	aen nistwayr	Then and there	ekoushpee pi ekota
Storyteller	flesheur, a teller of "tall tales." Translated into English, the closest	Then	akoushpee
		There	ekouta (close by)
		There	ikotay (over there)

There	naytay (way over there)
Thigh	la fess
Think	itayyihta
Thirteen	trayz
Thirty	trawnt
This	awa (for nouns which are animate) eg. Enn patak ana (This is a potato)
This	ooma (ouma) for nouns which are inanimate. Eg. Enn shezh ooma (This is a chair). Oumshee-shi (like this)
Thong (leather)	babiche
Thousand	mil
Threat	ekota tashi
Three	trwaw
Throttle	aen throttle
Thumb	li pous (poos)
Thursday	zhweejee
Tit(bird)	aen nwayzoo
Toad	aen krapoo
Toast	lee tous, en toast
Today	anoush
Toe	aen nartay, aen zartay
Toes	lee zartay
Toilet	la klawzet
Tomato	enn tomat
Tomatoes	lee tomat
Tomorrow	dimaen
Tongue	la or ta lawng (language)
Too	meena (also), nishta (me too)
Tooth	enn dawn
Toothpicks	li bois di dawn
Trap	aen pyeezh
Trapper	aen sasoer kaw ouhpayekayt
Tree	aen arbr
Tripe	li dibree
Tripe dish	la pawns or li dibree
Tripod	aen tripyee
Trousers	la kilot
Trout	la trut
Truck	aen trok
True	tawpway
Tub	enn cheuv
Tuesday	marjee
Turkey hen	enn daend
Turkey tom	aen gwadaend
Turtle	li torcheu
Twenty	vaen
Two	deu

U

Umbrella	an parapluee
Uncle	mon nook
Undershirt	en shmeezh ditsoor
Underwear	li bitaen ditsoor
Unfold	tshwaykinamihk
Unintentional	nmoo oushchitow
Unnecessary	nmoo katawt
Untie	apihkouna
Us	kiyanawn
Used to	mawna

V

Varicose	lee groos venn
Vegetables	lee zhardinaezh
Veil	enn wel
Velvet	li vloor
Vermillion	varmiyoon
Very	nawshpit, mitouni
Vest	enn vest
Veterans	lee vyeu soldaw
Vinegar	li vinaegr
Violet	vyalet
Violin	aen vyeloon
Visit	keewkayhk
Visitor	aen visitoer, keewkayshk (visits all the time)

W

Wagon	aen wawgoon
Wake up	koushkoupayi
Walk	pimoostayhk
Wall	la meurawy, li meur
Wall-eyed	napatayshkawpiw
Warm	kshitayw
Wart	aen cheehcheekoum
Wash (clothes)	kisheepaykinikay
Wash your body	kisheepaykee
Wash your face	kawsheekway
Wash	kisheepaykina
Washer	aen moulaen a lavee
Water	diloo
Waterhole	aen troo deau
Wave	wawshtahikayhk
We	niyanawn (you not included), kiyanawn (you included)
Wear	mishka
Weasel	enn blet
Weather	li tawn, enshikeeshikawk
Wedding	enn nos, aen maryaezh
Wednesday	mikarjee
Week	enn smenn

Wellmade	miyeushchikawtayw	Wrong	No kwayyesh
Werewolf	roogaroo	**X**	
What for	tawnayhki	**Y**	
What	kaykwawy	Yank	shashekwat ouchipita, shashekwat weekoupehtah,
Whatever	pikou ishi		
Wheat	li blee		
When	tashpee, ishpee	Yard	li tayraen alawntour la maezoon, la koor
Whenever	pakowishpee		
Where	tawnday	Yarn	li fil a lenn (as in wool)
Whether	keeshpin	Yawn	Tawatik
Which	tawnima	Year	Aen naw
White birch	li bouloo blawn	Yell	Taypway
White	blawn	Yellow	zhounn
Who is this	awana awa	Yellowish	nawutchikou zhounn
Who	awana, awina	Yes	wee, aenhen
Why	tawnayhki	Yesterday	iyayr
Wigwam	lozh	Yet	awshameena, keeyawpit (future), chayshkwa (not yet)
Wild turnip	lee navoo		
Willow	li soul		
Win	Pashkiyawkayw	Yolk	li zhounn daef
Window glass	la vitr di sawsee (shawsee)	You	kiya, kiyawow (all of you)
Window	Aen sawsee, aen shawsee	Young	Zhenn
		Your	Too, toon
Windy	yootin	Yours	kiyawnow, kiyawow anima
Wine	li vaen		
Wing	en zel	Yourselves	Kiyawow
Winter	l'ivayr	Youth	lee zhenn
Winter hat	aen shapoo d'ivayr	**Z**	
Wipe	kawsheena	Zeal	nouhtay
Wire	li wire	Zigzag	wawwush kamoun
With	avik	Zip	vif
Wolf	aen loo	Zipper	kepoupichikun awn fayr
Wolverine	weehtikouhkawn	Zoom	awmachiwaychaham
Womb	La matris		
Wood	li bwaw		
Wooden spoon	enn chouyayr en bwaw		
Wool	la lenn		
World	la tayr		
Worm	aen vayr		
Wren	Aen portifeu		
Write	Oushpayhikay		

Prayers and Invocations
Norman Fleury
Generic Prayer

Li Bon Jeu, not Createur, li kourawch miyinawn, paray chee itayhtamawk, kwayesh kapimouhtayhk, marsee chee itwayak ka kishcheetayimoyak.

God, Our Creator, give us courage, let us be of one mind, make us righteous, thankful and proud.

Lee Michif Weechihik awnsawmbl chee atoushkaychik, sourtoo lee vyeu chee awpachihayakouhk li zhen chee kishnamawachik pour li tawn ki vyaen.

Help the Métis to work together especially utilizing our Elders as teachers and preparing our youth for the future.

Li Bon Jeu la direksyoon miyinawn, itayha chimiyouitayhtamak, li shmaen chee oushtawyawk pour la Nawsyoon dee Michif ota dans not Piyee.

Lord provide us with direction and inspiration as we build a road for the Métis Nation in this Country.

Sa prawn lee famee di Michif chee shoohkshichik kishpin la Nasyoo di Michif chee shoohkawk.

We must have strong Métis families in order to have a strong Métis Nation.

Marsee ditwnanan.
Thank you and Amen.

Louis Riel Commemoration Service
Prayer

Li Bon Jeu, not Createur, tout li ans la Nasyoo d'Michif, not parawntee enawn, not zamee, lee zhenn, pi lee vyeu nakishkatowawk chee nakatweymachik pi marsee chee tweyhk a Louis Riel, not shef, pi lee Michif, kah kee shoohkee tawpwaytakihk, chee nootinikaychik, pour la Nasyoo d'Michif akoushpee, anoush, pi toul tawn.

Lord, God our Creator, every year on this day, we the Métis Nasyoo, our relatives, our friends, our youth and Elders, meet to remember and give thanks to Louis Riel, our leader, and the Métis people who believed in the cause of the Métis Nation, then, today, and always.

Louis Riel pi see Michif ka kee pimichishahou kout li shmenn kee oushistawawk pour la Nasyoo d'Michif anoush pi tout lee zoot Nasyoo li bon temp chee ayachik, katipaymishouchik, chimiyayhtakihk aen pimawtihichik dawn not bel province pi not payee ka katawshishik li Canada ka anishnikateyk.

Louis Riel and his Métis followers built the road for the Métis Nation and all other Nations so that we can enjoy freedom and good life in this great province of Manitoba, and the beautiful country called Canada.

Li Bon Jeu, anoush kishkishinawn ki moushoumipeninan, not soldawinan, pour leu sakrifis, aen ki li braev owochik kamaen kishpin chi nipouchik.

Today, Lord, we remember our forefathers, our Métis war veterans, for their sacrifices and their bravery, at all cost.

Li Bon Jeu ki kakwaychimiti nan dawn L'ispree di Louis Riel pi ni moushoumipeninan li kourawch ka miyikawshouyak li shimaen chee pimichichishawmawk kaw kee oushitawchik pi chee ahkamaymouyak.

Lord, we ask in the spirit of Louis Riel and of our Métis forefathers, to give us courage so we may remain on the road which they built and may uphold their visions.

Li Bon Jeu, kahkiyuw awiya ka shawkihat, kahkiyuw ki papainawn, marsee pour not tawn pawsee, marsee aen ki miyyawk la vee.

God of love, Father of us all, we thank You for our past, we thank you for creating us.

Li Bon Jeu, kwaychimitinawn toul tawn neekawneeshtamonawn niyanawn la Nasyoo d'Michif avik toon l'ispree d'amoor tou li tau li wayaezh Louis Riel ka kee mawchistawt chi pimichishahamawk.

We ask you God to continue to guide the Métis Nation with your spirit of love so we can continue our journey as Louis Riel would have wished.

Li Bon Jeu, Not Creatoer, li courage miyinawn, paray chee itayhtamawk, kwayesh kapimouhtayhk, marsee chee itwayak, ka kishcheetayimoyak.

God, our Creator, give us courage, let us be of one mind, make us righteous, thankful, and proud.

Lee Michif weechihik awnsawmbl chee atoushkaychik, sourtoo lee vyeu chee awpachihayakook li zhen chee kishnamawachik pour li tawn ki vyaen.

Help the Métis to work together especially utilizing our Elders as teachers and preparing our youth for the future.

Li Bon Jeu la direksyoon miyinawn itayhta chimiyouitayhtamak, li shmaen chee oushtawyawk pour la Nasyoo d'Michif ota dans not Piyee.

Lord provide us with direction and inspiration as we build a road for the Métis Nation in this country.

Sa praw lee famee di Michif chee shoohkshichik kispin la Nasyoo di Michif chee shoohkawk.

We must have strong Métis families in order to have a strong Métis Nation.

Marsee ditwnanan.

Thank you and Amen.

Glossary of Terms and Abbreviations

Adjective: A word or phrase naming an attribute. In English the adjective is added or grammatically related to a noun to modify or it or describe it.

Adverb: An adverb is a noun or phrase that modifies or quantifies another word (or word group) such as an adjective, verb or other adverb.

Agent: In an action expressed by a verb, the agent is the person to is actively involved in doing the action.

Animate: All objects and persons in Michif and Cree are either animate (roughly, living) or inanimate (roughly, lifeless, or without energy).

Conjunct Markers: Conjunct markers are grammatical items which serve to introduce subordinate (or "dependent") verbs or clauses.

Conjunct Mode: After a question word, like "why" or "when," and in the least central verb if there are two verbs in a sentence, then the verb given is given in the conjunct mode. The conjunct mode verb has the person markers only in the end of the verb

Consonants: The consonant is a speech sound in which the breath is at least partly obstructed. To form a syllable a consonant must be combined with a vowell

Direct: Each verb which has a subject that is more to the left in this schema than the object, has a direct marker in the verb: 2 > 1 > 3 > 4. Otherwise the verfb is inverse.

Ending: An element that is added to the end of a word, and that changes the use of the word, for example in English the plural ending of nouns -s (*joke, joke-s*) or the third person -s ("*(s)he thinks*").

Exclusive: Michif and many other languages (but not English) distinguish two kinds of "we": we including the speaker and "we" excluding the speaker. An example of exclusive "we" is: "we don't want you here." Here, "we" would be translated with *niyawnawn*.

First person: A grammatical term used for "I" and "me" in singular and "we, us" in plural.

Fourth person: A new person in a story. It is often marked with a special ending called obviative.

Grammar: Grammar is the system of rules for speaking and writing a language, e.g. word order, and word endings

Inclusive: Michif and many other languages (but not English) distinguish two kinds of "we": we including the speaker and "we" excluding the speaker. An example of inclusive "we" is: "Shall we go to your house?"

Independent mode: When there is only one verb in a sentence, it is a form of the independent mode.

Imperative: A form of the verb used for commands "go!" or for requests like "let us.... !"

Inflection: An inflection is an ending of a noun or a verb that has no meaning in itself (e.g. English -s), but it has some grammatical Inflection meanings for the sentence. For example *walk-s*. Inflectional elements in Cree are for example the person markers ni- and ki- and the direct/inverse endings.

Intransitive: A verb with no object is intransitive. With an object it is transitive.

Inverse: Each verb where the subject precedes the object in this schema, gets an inverse marker in the verb: 2 > 1> 3> 4. Otherwise the verb is direct.

Lexicon: A lexicon is a stock of words.

Morphology: The internal structure of words. The study and description of the word forming elements and processes of language such as; inflection, derivation and compounding.

Object: If there are two nouns in a sentence, the least central of these is the object. Usually that is the patient of an action, but in a passive sentence the patient become subject.

Obviative: When there are more than two third persons (he, she) in a story, the one that is least central in the story ("the other") can get a special ending called obviative. This is also marked in the verb.

Orthography: This refers to spelling conventions.

Patient: The patient of an action is the second noun used with a verb. It is the person or object that undergoes the action. The agent is the one that executes an action.

Person: A technical term for the person who acts or who is acted upon as expressed in a verb. See first person, second person, third person.

Phoneme: A phoneme is any of the units of sounds in a specified language that distinguish one word from another.

Phonetics: This refers to possible sounds and sound patterns - vocal sounds and their classification..

Phonics: This is a method of teaching reading by associating letters or groups of letters with particular sounds.

Phonography: Phonography relates to the sounds of speech. Phonology refers to the system of speech sounds. Michif is mixed in all respects except one—its phonological system. Its phonology consists of two separate systems, one for the Cree part and one for the French part. These systems do not influence each other at all. English elements are phonologically adjusted toward the French component, never toward the Cree.

Phonology: This term refers to distinctive sounds and sound patterns.

Plural: If there are lots of people or of things, it is a plural noun. Verbs in Cree and Michif are different depending on the plural.

Pragmatics: This term refers to the interpretation of utterances, language use.

Prefix: An element with some grammatical meaning attached to the front of a word stem.

Preposition: A preposition is a word governing, and usually preceding, a noun or pronoun and expressing a relation to another word, as in: 'the plate *on* the table."

Postposition: A postposition is a word or particle placed after the word it modifies for example, *ward* in *westward*.

Pronoun: A pronoun is a word used instead of and to indicate a noun already mentioned or known, for example, *we*, *this* or *ourselves*.

Second person: The person one speaks to, i.e. "you"

Semantics: the meanings of words and sentences.

Singular: If there is only one of something, it will be expressed in singular in a language.

Subject: The main noun in a sentence, usually the agent. In a passive sentence the patient is subject.

Suffix: An element with some grammatical meaning attached after a word stem.

Syllable: A syllable is a unit of pronounciation uttered without interruption. Syllables usually have one vowel sound often with a consonant or consonants before and after.

Syntax: the ways in which words are combined.

Tilde: The tilde is a mark placed over a letter eg. Over a Spanish *n* when it is to be pronounced *ny*, as in *señor* or a Potuguese *a* or *o* when they are nasalized as in *São Paulo*.

Third person: Neither the speaker, nor the hearer, but a third person, or a thing.

Transitive: A verb with an object is intransitive. Without an object a verb is transitive.

Verb: A verb is the word in a sentence that expresses a state or an action.

Vowel: A vowel is a speech sound made with vibration of the vocal cords, but without audible friction. A vowel is more open than a consonant and a single vowel can form a syllable.

Word Formation: how words are made from more basic elements

Abbreviations

VAI	Abbreviation for animate intransitive verb: people or animals do something that does not effect others, e.g. sleep, walk, be tired, dance, etc.
VII	Abbreviation for inanimate intransitive verb: these verbs say something about non-living things, e.g. that it is clean, it happens, it snows, it runs along, it exists, etc.

Section 1: What does the literature say about major factors that impact the success of second language instruction?

Much second language instruction focuses on teaching children as the best way to assure true successful acquisition of a second language, specifically where young children are completely immersed in the second language, and the target language is also the language of instruction. The most successful language revitalization programs (Maori and Hawaii) use language-nesting programs with young children. However, it is not sufficient for only children to speak the language. Fishman (1991) stresses that for successful language revitalization, *intergenerational* communication must be targeted. Today, it is often only the elders who are fluent speakers of indigenous languages, and the focus is on teaching the next generation of children, but it is important not to forget the 'lost' generation: adults who now often have children who could be learning the language in school. These children would have no one to speak it with outside the school situation, creating an artificial, or at least restricted setting for the language. Members of this 'lost' generation have for the most part lost their indigenous languages due to language policies and/or dominant language, and this is the case around the world. In order for any long-term revitalization to take place, there must be a stream of teaching adults as well as a stream of teaching children. In fact, a third stream is necessary: one in which the fluent elders are instructed in linguistics and second-language instruction. The two latter streams: teaching adults and teaching teachers are the focus of this report. Aside from recognizing that children must be part of any goal towards greater language revitalization, I will set children's instruction aside for the time being in order to focus on adult language instruction.

Successful methods of adult second language teaching

Two methods of language teaching advocated by the indigenous second-language literature (and by second language instructors in general) are Total Physical Response (TPR) and language immersion programs. Below I give excerpts from Ignace (1998) outlining these two methodologies.

Total Physical Response

Total Physical Response (TPR), originally developed by James Asher in the United States.

Some of its principles are:
- second language learning is based on the pattern of first language acquisition. Students learn listening, speaking, reading and writing in that order. Language learning is more successful if words and phrases are learned through action. Its basic procedure is as follows:
- teacher demonstrates a task - students listen and respond to commands by following the teacher's modeling;
- instructor repeats the commands and models them with a small group of students, then one student;
- instructor adds new commands and combines new and old commands with entire group, then small groups;
- instructor recombines old and new commands without modeling, and group responds, and individuals respond;
- Later (after 10 hours), teacher reverses roles and students give commands.

TPR can work well in teaching actions and actions combined with vocabulary. With a skillful and trained teacher, the TPR approach can also teach grammatical concepts, many of them with the help of games and routines. TPR, in a wider sense, is an inventory of user-friendly drills and exercises which help students develop listening skills, and if the approach is followed with care, speaking skills, as well. [Ignace 1998, chapter 8]

Language immersion programs:

Like language nests, immersion programs at the Kindergarten through Grade 12 level (K-12) are modelled on the advantage of "natural acquisition" of a language through maximum exposure, modelling, and repetition, as opposed to learning a second language through drills, formal memorizing and grammatical explanations. The immersion approach has been widely practised in Canada with French immersion (Programme Cadre francais) during the last 20 years. According to the immersion approach, all school activities and all instruction from Kindergarten throughout the primary years are carried out in the language that is to be learned (the "target language").

Since French immersion has become widespread in Canada, there has been much debate among language educators about the effectiveness of the immersion approach. At first glance, immersion seems to be an ideal solution, which leads to excellent listening skills (comprehension) and excellent speaking skills (expression) in the target language, through seemingly effortless prolonged exposure. Immersion children appear to have good comprehension, and are able to speak with much more ease and far less inhibition in a shorter period of time.

On closer inspection, however, it is important to realize that a classroom immersion situation is not a "natural acquisition" situation. The teacher, who is either a native speaker of the second language or very proficient in it but also knows English, uses the language to communicate with a large number of children who are already proficient in English and will want to use English with each other out of habit. The teacher then has to maintain communication in the second language (whether French or an Aboriginal language) in the face of children who have an urge to talk English to one another and to the teacher. It takes a competent immersion teacher more than a year to enforce the use of the target language with the teacher; it usually takes some years to enforce the use in the classroom among students, and, usually, the use of the target language does not carry forth to the playground and to activities or conversation among students outside of the classroom unless incentives and rewards for this are established. Critics of French immersion have also pointed out that, while immersion students have excellent comprehension skills, their speaking skills are by no means perfect. Immersion students can express themselves fluently in French, but their spoken French, after years of modelling by teachers, often has an English accent and is grammatically flawed, in that it shows a large influence by English.

> [...] for the sake of preserving an Aboriginal language, it is important that children who become competent in the language will use it with each other outside of the classroom, with elders in their community, and with their own children as they grow up and become parents. Many elders also feel that it is important that young people who learn their Aboriginal language learn how to pronounce the often difficult sounds to the fullest extent possible, and learn to preserve the richness of the grammar and its nuances of meaning by eventually *mastering* the language. Because of their shortcomings, French immersion programs have recently put emphasis on students learning phonetically and grammatically correct speech by combining the exposure to the language with more formal methods of teaching the language, such as drills, grammatical explanations, and correcting the speech and writing of students. These seem to have improved the speech and writing of French immersion students. [Ignace 1998, Chapter 7]

Note that one thing these two methods share is the emphasis on *communication* and *participation* of language learners. Second language teaching literature overwhelmingly advocates focusing on *communicative* aspects of language, rather than on grammatical or vocabulary aspects, in order to assure real success. This means that any successful program will entail students speaking in real-life situations which are relevant to them, rather than simply listening, repeating grammar drills or vocabulary, or memorizing. Next I will give an overview of a successful adult language learning program that was developed by the Native California Network in 1992 primarily by Leanne Hinton, Nancy Richardson and Mary Bates Abbott, and which has been quite successful. This program, called the Master-Apprentice program, was modeled on the above approaches to second language teaching and applied to adult learners.

Master/Apprentice program:

California's Master-Apprentice Language Learning Program is a program that teaches native speakers and young adults to work together intensively so that the younger members may develop conversational proficiency in the language. It is designed to be a one-on-one relationship between the "master" (speaker) and the "apprentice." (language learner) The main principles of the program are as follows:

- No English is allowed: the master speaker must try to use his language at all times while with the apprentice, and the apprentice must use the language to ask questions or respond to the master (even if he or she can only say 'I don't understand')
- The apprentice must be at least as active as the master in deciding what is to be learned and in keeping communication going in the language • The primary mode of transmission and learning is always oral, not written.
- Learning takes place primarily in real-life situations, such as cooking, washing clothes, gardening, taking walks, doing crafts, going to traditional ceremonies, and so on.
- The activity itself along with other forms of nonverbal communication will provide the context in which the language can be understood by the beginning learner. [Hinton 2001:218]

Each program is meant to run for 360 hours of language immersion work, and the apprentice must keep a lot of their work describing their activities. After each 40 hours, a log is sent into the coordinator. Each participant receives a stipend of $3000 for his/her participation, and this is distributed based on 40-hour periods, sent after the log is received. Each team receives a weekend-long initial training, but the work is done mostly alone, given scattered geographic circumstances. Principles of immersion showing skills of nonverbal communication and language teaching through commands are discussed during the training session to get the pair comfortable with not using English, as well as teaching methods for communication they will need to use.

Once the initial training is complete, apprentices set up appointments to spend time with their masters learning in real-life situations, such as making dinner and setting tables, fishing, shopping, etc. During these meetings, no English is allowed, and both members of the team must endeavour to speak and communicate as much as possible. This program has been quite successful in training young professional-age adults in the language so that they can in turn teach it themselves: many apprentices have gone on to become language teachers. A total of 65 teams have gone through the program, and twenty different languages have been taught. For more complete discussion of the Master-Apprentice program, see Hinton (1997), Hinton (2001), Hinton et al. (2002). Leanne Hinton is well-known for her work in endangered language teaching, and is a leading expert on the subject, having written many language learning and teaching manuals and papers directed primarily at indigenous languages.

One of the excellent aspects about the Master-Apprentice program is how it is designed to use language for a *purpose*. The lessons are less targeted at particular aspects of language and more towards setting up relationships and real-life situations where it is necessary to communicate. Even in the absence of such a program, however, it is possible to incorporate some of the key components of this type of program's success into a classroom setting. In the next section, I will outline various factors raised as important in second language teaching classes, which should be considered when setting up adult Michif language classes.

i. Using the target language as the language of instruction: keep English out of the classroom.

It is generally accepted that the best way to teach a language involves the teacher and students being *actively involved* in the learning process. Instead of setting up classes in English to teach another language's grammar and vocabulary, basing it on English, using the language in all aspects of classroom activities is crucial. This entails use by the teacher of non-oral communication such as gestures, pictures, miming, etc., in order to make oneself understood.

ii. Base teaching materials around situational, commnication-based learning.

Any teacher of an indigenous language will be primarily on their own in terms of lesson planning, as there are very limited resources available. It is important to plan out what one plans to accomplish in each lesson. There are three different ways in which to plan lessons: based on vocabulary, grammar or situations. One recurring pitfall indigenous language lessons display, for example, is that they are based solely around vocabulary, rather than on communication. Hinton argues that language teachers should use all three approaches, focusing especially on situation planning, which is the most fruitful of the three strategies. For the purposes of exposition, I outline here how these three different language-planning methods work (or don't work).

The most common method for basing lessons with novice teachers is one based on vocabulary.[12] Across many different endangered language communities, the traditional strategy in language classes has been to teach lists of words. However, this is not productive in making students actually use the language for (at least) three reasons. First, teaching around vocabulary is very limiting in terms of inspiration. Second, these word lists tend to consist primarily of nouns and some verbs or fixed expressions. This lends itself to naming tasks, but does not constitute using language in any communicative form. Communication is the primary reason people use language, and so tasks dealing with non-communicative functions of language are frustrating to students who do not find occasion to simply name entities. Lastly, though related, there is no way to use these words in a thought or sentence, and so the language 'knowledge' the students have acquired has little to nothing to do with grammar and the actual language structure: it is simply a memorized set of words which do not link up in any way. Note that this is the method used by indigenous language teachers across the world, to no fault of their own. These teachers are highly motivated fluent speakers, but usually have no language training or knowledge about language acquisition. Most people of all linguistic backgrounds equate language with vocabulary and spelling, and so it is not surprising that this is how non-linguistically trained people would teach their language.

Other second language classes have focused on grammar instruction, recognizing that grammar is important to being able to formulate sentences. This, however, like classes based on vocabulary, is of limited productivity. First, classes taught on the basis of grammar also often result in memorization of structures, like the vocabulary strategy, where students simply memorize conjugations. Again, though this is somewhat more useful than just learning individual words, there is no context, and no communicative function to memorized verb paradigms/conjugations, and can be frustrating when the student goes to try to form a sentence in

---

[12] Note that all current Michif lessons available are based around vocabulary.

the language. Further, as Hinton reports, grammars differ from language to language, and it is important to think about the language in question when teaching grammar. For example, some languages have different tenses, other have suffixes not present in English. In Michif, for example, there are two types of 'we' – a first person plural *exclusive* form, which does not include the hearer, and a first person plural *inclusive* form, which does include the hearer. Teaching from a purely grammatical point of view can be difficult because the teacher needs to think about the particular grammar in question. This is not impossible, but it is more difficult.

The most fruitful method of language teaching, according to Hinton, is to think in terms of situations. One important reason for this is that each community shares different heritage activities and traditions, and there is a special vocabulary for those traditions which can be taught by means of situational language. Alana Johns, in a personal communication, advises to keep the language relevant to the particular community, and to specifically ask them what they want to learn how to say. This situational method lends itself to meeting that goal. People want to learn how to speak a language in order to use it in certain settings, normally. If the language teaching methodology is adapted for these settings, the students will be more interested, motivated, and prone to use the language.

In drawing up lesson plans based on this situational use, the instructor or curriculum designer should think about the vocabulary and grammar necessary for reaching the particular goals of the situation. For example, a lesson could be planned around a cooking lesson, where the vocabulary goals would include food and kitchen words, and the grammar goals would be to learn to give orders (imperatives). Another could be based on what one did last summer, which could have leisure activities as vocabulary goals, and the use of the past tense as grammatical goals. Therefore, though the situational method is the most learner-friendly, and the most fruitful in terms of motivating students, it should not be used in a void: careful consideration of both vocabulary and grammar is necessary when designing a lesson. Often these lessons can be taught by means of a dialogue which students can mimic, and then new vocabulary is brought in, and students may apply new vocabulary what they've learnt. Note that I am not advocating keeping grammar out of the classroom. Quite the contrary: adult learners want to understand grammatical concepts. However, grammar should be introduced as *necessary background material* needed for communication in the given situation; it should not be the end to the lesson in of itself.

Approaches to Lesson Planning
Table 14.1 in Hinton (2001), p185)

Vocabulary	**Grammar**	**Situations**
Numbers Colors Kinship terms Animals Plants Clothing Seasons, months, days Weather and astronomical terms Kitchen utensils Household objects Actions (stand, walk, give…) (etc.)	Plurals Past, present, future Case (object, subject, etc.) Adjectives Word order Transitive and intransitive verbs Irregular verbs (etc.)	*Everyday life:* Greeting people, Shopping, Talking on a phone, Planting garden, Cooking, Driving a car *Traditional life:* Language usage for a particular ceremony, Traditional crafts, Prayer, Traditional medicine, Traditional cooking *School life:* Sharing, Reading and writing, Math, history and other subjects, Hanging up coat Washing hands, Using bathroom, Snack time, Playground activities (etc.)

A good, trained language teacher should take care to prepare lesson plans chronologically to ensure that students are learning cumulatively in terms of grammar and vocabulary, and so each lesson touches on a new grammatical concept.

iii. Comprehension precedes production

Students should be expected to understand before being able to produce language. To that end, beginning classes should be focussed more on having students follow instructions, and then move to students repeating language constructions, and gradually to actual production.

iv. Repetition and reinforcement

It is said that students need to hear new vocabulary or a new structure twenty times in twenty different situations before it will be really learned. Note that this does not simply mean repeating a word twenty times, but actually *using* the word twenty times. This translates into ensuring that there is a review component at the beginning of classes, or at least at some point during the class, rather than simply introducing new vocabulary or concepts and expecting students to absorb them and be able to use them creatively.

v. Community consultation.

In speaking with linguists involved in language revitalization programs, one recurring recommendation was to consult with the community in questions before setting up a program. The common sense here is that if the community isn't interested or engaged in the lesson plan, motivation to learn will fade quickly. The best way to ensure motivation is to ask the members themselves what they want to learn. For example, young people in Alana Johns' classes in Labrador wanted especially to communicate with their grandparents. This should of course be encouraged, and class situations can be tailored to teach vocabulary, phrases and necessary grammatical structures to appropriate situations when it is known what students want to learn. In this vein, lessons should be relevant to the particular traditions and culture, and in this way, culture is taught alongside and as part of language. There is little value in teaching names of oceanic animals and methods of crab trapping, for example, in a fishing class taking place in the Canadian Prairies. Related to the community, it is important to set up programs based on a 'bottom-up' approach, meaning look to community members and build a program based on the abilities of the capable and motivated members, rather than a 'top-down' approach, where an ambitious program is designed and then one goes out looking for someone to implement it. This is simply a waste of resources when there is no one capable of implementation, based either on fluency, resources, availability or interest.

vi. Encouragement rather than criticism.

Adults tend to be nervous to make mistakes, and don't want to practice. Teacher should make sure students are encouraged to speak and not be afraid of mistakes. Criticism is the quickest way to discourage students of any age, and so praise and positive correction should be encouraged.

vii. If the goal is to develop oral competence, then the principal method of teaching should be oral.

Many language classes focus on reading and writing as part of the curriculum. Although literacy is encouraged, if, after community consultation, the goal is to develop oral competence,

The main threat of dialect differences is that they create a division between speakers when these speakers should be working together. As Ignace suggests, focusing on similarities rather than differences is preferable to avoid division. Indeed, the differences should be thought of as evidence of the richness of the language, rather than used as a division between people. In the Michif case, it should be clear to teachers (and students) that differences in dialects are normal and present in all languages of the world, and perhaps can even be incorporated into lessons at some stage. This can be important with respect to avoiding community factionalization, which is the next barrier to a successful language learning program discussed.

iii. Community factionalization and lack of support for efforts;

One of the major barriers to any language revitalization project has nothing to do with any technical aspects of the task: all the planning and good intentions in the world can be undermined by the human factor. Specifically, any splits in the community based on philosophy or control can have a devastating effect on any progress. For example, though Hawaii is touted as a success story overall, No'eau Warner (2001) describes a split within one of the communities where half the students have been taken out of the Hawaiian immersion school and were taught in a park with no books or paid teachers, while the other half stayed in the school. OnNo'eau Warner describes this split as a struggle for power, where one group rejects another group being in charge of their school. These are the types of problems which can arise which are the hardest to circumvent, as it involves personalities, but they can also be the most damaging to efforts. Language revitalization takes an extraordinary amount of work, and will only succeed with co-operation between people in the community. The Michif community has an added difficulty in terms of potential community factionalization not seen in other indigenous communities with regards to the language issue. Most communities associate a particular language to their culture, even if that language is made up of different dialects. Due to the creation of a new culture and nation through other cultures, there is no single language, associated with the Métis community: French, English, Michif, Saulteaux and Cree could all be thought to be Métis languages. This creates a division along language lines unattested in other communities. When putting resources into the maintenance of one of the Métis languages, in this instance, Michif, it is likely that speakers of other Métis languages will ask why their own language is not receiving the same amount of attention. Given the larger picture, it would be counter-productive to completely ignore Métis French (or Cree, or Saulteaux) as a Métis language, especially given its status as a minority language. The difference, however, is that French as a language is not in severe danger of disappearing, and even Cree and Saulteaux are not in as dire a situation as Michif. There are French speakers all over the world, and although the Métis dialect is unique, it is not in the same state of decline as Michif. Members of both language communities must be engaged together to see the larger picture of maintaining *all* Métis languages as part of their heritage, and be focused together on the more pressing needs of putting more resources into Michif, while continuing to encourage the speaking of French to children at home. It is my understanding that within the Métis French speaking community, while there is a decline in French usage, French is still being spoken in many homes. In the case of Cree and Saulteaux, it would be advisable to band with First Nations groups to encourage the continued speaking of these languages. Again, there are still speakers of different ages speaking the language. Of course, there is a real danger that this will not continue if the community is not vigilant, but even this is not the case for Michif. It is important for all Métis people to recognize the seriousness of the state of the decline of Michif, and be on board with efforts in order for real progress to be made.

It is not sufficient, however, simply to maintain peace between communities. Rather, communities should be active participants in any plan, and should have continued input and updates, so as to be as transparent as possible, to avoid future problems, but also, for maximum benefit of revitalization programs. Community consultation was mentioned in section 1 with regards to teaching with students' wishes in mind, and this is much the same idea. If the community has input into the curriculum, presumably they will be more attached to it, and more motivated. Motivation and excitement for learning is the most intangible, but very important factor in indigenous language teaching. Students who feel they have some say in their education, and who are getting what they want out of the program are much more likely to succeed. As a result, it is important to consult *with* the community to arrive at the best results *for* the community.

iv. Stability in funding and personnel;

Available, stable resources are an ever-present problem when dealing with programs of instruction of an endangered language. Resources include both human and financial. First, in terms of human resources, it is widely recommended to have a critical mass, normally *at least three trained speakers* of the language responsible for language policy and planning. Having a single person responsible is not advisable for two main reasons: first, it is a tremendous burden for a single person to bear, and second, a wide variety of personal reasons can make it that the single individual is no longer able to assume the responsibility. It is short-sighted to think that one person may single-handedly be responsible for all language policy, curriculum development, documentation and teaching, for example. Financial resources are an obvious problem when dealing with programs of revitalisation: hiring people costs money, and in these cases, it is not enough to simply pay language speakers to be teachers. The speakers themselves need to be trained in linguistics and language pedagogy and time must be spent on developing curriculum and reference materials. Many language revitalization projects are just that: projects, with a limited time for limited funds. Ideally, a permanent administrative committee, department or language authority should be established to assure continuity of funds and vision for the future of the language.

v. Lack of long-term vision for classes

Language classes need to be organized in a way that learners are inspired and can see progress. Lack of any vision or continuity of classes is a major factor in the abandonment of any class, but is especially noticeable in language classes. Consider the following quote:

> Many language teachers themselves, as well as parents and speakers, have bemoaned this difficulty, and have made reference to an "endless loop of colours, numbers and animals." Since action commands ("sit," "stand up," "walk," "turn around") and body parts, as well as numbers, basic colour terms and animal words are relatively easy concepts to teach at least superficially many language teachers begin by teaching them. Then, year after year, these themes are repeated without the introduction of much new subject matter. [Ignace 1998]

The very commissioning of this report is an attempt to avoid this lack of vision, of course, but it is something to be aware of as a problem affecting many communities and many languages classes (be they indigenous or non-indigenous) taught by non-trained language teachers around the world. This lack of vision is often directly related to the lack of language pedagogy training, which is the last potential problem addressed in this section.

vi. Lack of training for language teachers.

Lastly, a serious problem with adult indigenous language programs deals directly with the lack of trained language teachers conducting classes. Many language classes are run by fluent speakers lacking linguistic and pedagogical training, which seriously hinders the progress which can be made. A crucial step in any successful language teaching program must be to set up standards which must be met by any language instructor. These may take the form of official qualifications, which is ultimately the preferred solution, to legitimize the teachers in the eyes of the students, in the eyes of government bodies, and even in the eyes of the teachers themselves. Many speakers turned teachers do so from extreme dedication and good will to prevent their language from disappearing, but they themselves are not necessarily confident in their teaching abilities, and validation from external sources and education can play an important role towards gaining confidence. They, themselves know they are not necessarily equipped to teach their language. Alternatively, they are confident but do not realize what training they require, and as a result think that simply by speaking a few words in a class, or giving vocabulary, they are teaching their language, which an equally problematic circumstance. Consider the following, issued from the American Indian Languages Institute, which since 1978 has provided training in language instruction in the American Southwest:

1. We cannot teach language simply because we are speakers of that language. We must know what our language is like - its structure and function in everyday existence.
2. Even when we know these things about our language, we cannot teach it effectively. We need to know how our language may be acquired by our children. If we know the process we have a better framework with which we can develop curriculum and teaching materials.
3. We need to know what a curriculum should include, in what sequence and how much... We must emphasize how we use our language if that language is to be useful. We therefore, do not teach a language just as an academic subject: We teach language as part of our total existence and as a basis for meaningful existence.

(Watahomigie and Yamamoto 1992, quoted in Fettes 1992 and Ignace 1998)

What do language teachers need to know in order to become effective adult language teachers? The following list, adapted from Ignace (1998) (and supplemented) covers the ideal situation:

- An understanding of the process of language acquisition and language learning;
- An understanding of basic issues in language planning and language revitalization;
- An understanding of the use and development of effective and appropriate teaching strategies;
- An understanding and ability to use and develop language curriculum; • Capable of reading and writing the language to prepare and use instructional resources;
- An understanding of the connection between Aboriginal language and culture, in order to be able to teach the language as an integrated part of existence;
- An understanding of dialect differences and ability to incorporate this knowledge into the classroom.

The problem, then, lies in *how* to train future language teachers. Some university programs have been developed, (Simon Fraser University has an eight-course certificate in First Nations Language Proficiency[14] and Memorial University of Newfoundland runs a program for Labrador Inuttut and Innu-aimun, for example, and University of Victoria is also involved in similar efforts) to teach a cohort of students about their language, linguistics and to train future indige-

---

[14] Courses in other locations and/or in other languages can be offered at the request of the First Nations communities/organizations. The certificate consists of 27 credit hours of course work. Eighteen of these credit hours must be earned by completing beginner and intermediate level courses in the aboriginal language itself. Six of the credit hours involve courses in introductory linguistics and practical phonetics. The remaining courses include optional advanced courses in the language, descriptive linguistics of the same language, or course the aboriginal language teaching methodology, aboriginal language literature or aboriginal language curriculum development.

nous language teachers. While these are excellent opportunities, they are within the realm of a university setting, and may not always be the preferred method of the community. Note, however, that outreach programs in the communities themselves can be set up so that speakers do not have to travel to the university itself (though it is not clear that these programs could be set up in another province). It will be up to the community to decide whether it wants to pursue this avenue, to a more official qualification.

There should be someinvestigation on the feaibility of an independent stream of language teacher training specifically tailored to the Michif language for future Michif teachers. (Note that this could later be extended to Cree and/or Saulteaux if desired.) These courses may or may not be tied to a local university or community college, but a linguist and/or a language pedagogy specialist should be responsible for course/program design and instruction, incorporating the points above into the required curriculum for future language teachers. The speakers should be able to take these courses free of charge (and even be paid if possible, as incentive) but it should be mandatory for future language instructors to have gone through the training before having their own class to teach.

Because this training takes time, and we are in a race against time to start teaching the language, it may be desirable to have linguist and speaker develop course materials together concurrent with this training, and have them both in the classroom together as co-teachers. This is beneficial to both parties: the linguist learns how to speak the language (and not simply record its structure) and the speaker learns the technical information necessary with regards to pedagogy, linguistics, and curriculum design. The goal of course is that the speaker will become self-sufficient, and able to teach in the classroom on his/her own.

A co-teaching program has been developed by Alana Johns & Irene Mazurkewich in Labrador for Labrador Inuttut and Innu-aimun, and is outlined in the Hinton & Hale 2001 volume. This particular program taught fluent speakers aspects of linguistics, language, and language pedagogy in the context of a university setting. Then, these trained speakers taught university-level language courses in three stages. In stage one, the speakers co-taught as assistants to the linguists. They helped prepare language teaching materials and worked in the classroom, aiding the students in their pronunciation, while the linguist was in charge of the organization of the course, the preparation of materials, teaching, testing, and administrative duties. Mentoring was regarded as important because it allowed the student teachers to learn aspects of course materials preparation, to develop adult second-language teaching methodologies, and "especially to deliver courses at a level appropriate to university education.4" (Johns & Mazurkewich 2001:360) This first stage also allowed teaching assistants to gain confidence in the classroom, an underrated quality of any good teacher. The second stage was a reversal of the process, where the speaker became the principal instructor, and the linguist became the assistant, assisting in the preparation of course materials, helping students with pronunciation and consulting regarding marking and evaluation. The final stage intends the speaker to become the lecturer without the aid of the linguist. Note that speakers may go through stage 1 twice before moving on to stage two, etc. Such a program is a good model for getting non-trained teachers into the classroom and getting *on-the-job* training, and should be considered in the Michif case.

Conclusions: recommendations for best practices in program structure and teaching methods Michif beginner adult language classes.

Overall, my recommendations are to first establish a language authority including a number of Michif speakers, hopefully representing different dialects. This authority. Note that this is likely not a concern for Michif at the short term, but is worth thinking about for the future would be responsible for assuring the integrity of the materials developed and to develop a vision for the course after community consultation. Further, it is crucial to train teachers of Michif in some linguistics and pedagogy. This is of utmost importance to assure the success of the classes. My recommendation would also be to have a linguist or language pedagogue collaborate with the language authority in curriculum design, lesson planning, and for the classes to be co-taught by a speaker and a linguist both, especially in the first years of teaching. Once the teachers have undergone the training program and have co-taught at least one (preferably two) course(s), the linguist could be phased out of the classroom setting. In terms of classroom techniques, I would recommend that lessons revolve around communicative, situational learning, and that English not be used in the classroom whenever possible. See table 1 for ideas of lesson planning, and Appendix A for things to think about during curriculum development.

Recommendations for stages of action:

Stage 1: Appoint language planning authority
- community consultation to determine goals: what do learners want to learn? What is the goal in introducing Michif back into community?
- elders and future learners both should have input.
- assure that there are Michif speakers on the planning authority

Stage 2: Set up Michif language teacher training program. Program would include:
- issues in general linguistics, including language acquisition and language learning, language variation, basic concepts in phonology, morphology, syntax;
- issues in language planning and language revitalization;
- effective and appropriate teaching strategies;
- language curriculum development;
- connection between language and culture; Note that it may be possible to arrange help in this training with Simon Fraser University in Burnaby, B.C.

Stage 3 Design curriculum
- done by language authority and linguist together.
- see Appendix 1 for issues in curriculum design to be aware of.
- lesson plans should be designed based on communicative approach, around situations.

Stage 4 Develop resource materials (concurrently with stage 3, ongoing)
- outline grammatical rules, paradigms.
- make up dialogues, grammar exercises, etc.

Stage 5 Teach part 1 of course
- co-taught with linguist and language teacher.

Stage 6 Evaluation of part 1
- evaluate and incorporate any necessary changes before moving on to part 2 of course.
- develop curriculum, lesson plans for part 2.

Stage 7 Teach part 2 of course, develop more advanced courses, etc.

Ordering constraints of stages:
Stage 1 should be undertaken first, though may be concurrent with stage 2.
Stage 2 needs to be before stage 3 and 4, though an abbreviated training is possible in the interim if stage 5 includes team-teaching with a linguist.

Human resources recommendations:
Minimum:

- one linguist or language pedagogy expert to set up teacher training program, help with curriculum and resources development and to co-teach first classes.
- two (preferably three) speakers to assist with curriculum and resource development
- as many speakers as possible to go through language teaching training.

Notes on Contributors

Peter Bakker

Peter Bakker was recently working as a professor of linguistics at the Danish Institute for Advanced Studies in the Humanities in Copenhagen, Denmark. He has now returned to Aarhus University in Denmark where he previously taught. His Métis-specific book based on primary source material is *A Language of Our Own: The Genesis of Michif, the Mixed Cree-French Language of the Canadian Métis* (Toronto: Oxford University Press, 1997). This book is based on the almost ten years of research that went into his Ph.D. thesis of the same title. He wrote "The Michif Language of the Metis," for *Metis Legacy: A Metis Historiography and Annotated Bibliography* (Winnipeg: Pemmican Publications Inc, 2001).

Peter Bakker has published in numerous refereed journals. The Metis people generally credit Peter with bringing their language to Canadian and world attention. Peter Bakker and Norman Fleury have now completed *Learn Michif: Kishkeehta Michif.* (Authors, March 2004). This language CD is intended to assist the student to learn Michif by listening. There is an accompanying handbook.

Lawrence J. Barkwell

Lawrence Barkwell, an Honourary Life Member of the Manitoba Métis Federation; is employed as a Senior Policy Analyst in the Tripartite Self-Government Negotiations Department of Manitoba Metis Federation (MMF). He is on secondment from the Manitoba Aboriginal Affairs Secretariat to MMF. Lawrie has edited or co-edited six books, provided chapters for several textbooks and contributed articles to a variety of refereed journals. Three of his Métis specific titles are *The Struggle for Recognition: Canadian Justice and the Métis Nation* (with Sam Corrigan), *Past Reflects the Present: The Métis Elders' Conference* (with Fred Shore) and *Metis Legacy: A Metis Historiography and Annotated Bibliography* (with Leah Dorion and Darren Préfontaine). In December of 2002, this last book won the Saskatchewan Book Award for Publishing in Education. Over the last 25 years, Lawrie has taught at Brandon University (Winnipeg Centre Project), the Louis Riel Institute and Red River College. He is on the Board of Directors of Pemmican Publications, a non-profit Metis publishing house.

Rita Flamand

Rita Flamand is a Metis woman born at Camperville Manitoba. She is a mother, grandmother, and great grandmother. She is the daughter of Peter (Chi'pit) Flamand and Anne Fayant. Peter was born at St. John's, North Dakota (near Turtle Mountain); he was an excellent linguist and spoke Michif, French, English, Saulteaux and Ukrainian. Her mother was born in Camperville. Her maternal grandparents were Joseph Fayant and Catherine Chartrand. Catherine was from Montagne de Lim (File Hills). Her paternal grandparents were Joseph Flamand and Marie Thorn, both from Baie St. Paul, Manitoba. After the 1870 Resistance many Metis families had left Manitoba. Around 1887, the Flamands went to the U.S.A. where they had relatives and this is how her father came to be born in North Dakota.

For many years Rita has been concerned that the oral language of Michif as spoken at Camperville and area will become extinct before it is recorded in written form. For many years Rita has taught the Michif language at Camperville and at the Metis Resource Centre in Winnipeg. Rita herself is an excellent linguist and speaks, Michif, French, Plains Cree, Saulteaux and English. She is a graduate of the Michif Legal and Medical Translation course given by Red River College. She was an informant for Peter Bakker when he did his seminal study of the Michif language. Her Michif lessons appear on the Metis Resource Centre website (with streaming audio) and have served as the exposure of many people throughout the world to this unique language.

As a nurse, Rita moved around Manitoba and across the country from James Bay to Vancouver. She is a past president of the Metis Women's Association and had developed the Metis Academy a forerunner of the Louis Riel Institute. She also held appointment as a Magistrate in Camperville. Rita had eight children, her son Keiron is a noted Metis author, illustrator and artist.

In 1975, Rita was featured in the book, *Speaking Together: Canada's Native Women* (Ottawa: Secretary of State). Rita has been a role model, teacher, community volunteer and cultural preservationist for many years. In 2001, Rita provided the Michif translation for *Li Minoush*, written by Bonnie Murray. This book is part of Pemmican Publications *Michif Children's Series*. Rita's most recent publication is *Michif Conversational Lessons for Beginners* (Winnipeg: Metis Resource Centre. 2003).

Norman Fleury

Norman Fleury is the Director of the Manitoba Metis Federation Michif Languages Program and National; Co-chair of the Metis National Council's Michif Language Revitalization Program. Norman credits his 101-year-old mother and her mother with teaching him the importance of the Michif language. "When you went to her (grandmother's) place and spoke to her in English, she'd say speak to me in our language. I don't understand you. I'm not an English woman and my language is Michif.' My grandmother looked at our language as a spiritual language, a God given language."

Norman took teacher's training through the IMPACTE program offered by Brandon University. He was the director for the drug and alcohol abuse program of the Dakota Ojibway Tribal Council, a health liaison worker and a Life Skills Coach at the Oo-Za-We-Kwun Centre at Rivers, Manitoba. Norman has served as a Chairman of the MMF Local at St. Lazare and as an MMF director from Southwest Region. Besides French and English, Norman speaks seven of the Aboriginal languages common to the Metis. Norman is author of *La Lawng: Michif Peekishkwewin: The Canadian Michif Language Dictionary* (Winnipeg: Metis Resource Centre and Manitoba Metis Federation, 2000). Norman has a great love of horses and farms near Woodnorth in southwestern Manitoba.

Nicole Rosen

Nicole Rosen is a Ph.D. candidate at the University of Toronto, Department of Linguistics. Norman Fleury is her Michif language consultant. Her thesis is entitled "Domains in Michif Phonology." Her first major paper on Michif (2000) was "Non-Stratification in Michif." Her second paper, "Demonstrative Position in Michif" has been published in the *Canadian Journal of Linguistics*. She has also presented papers on the Michif language at various conferences and universities including *Workshops on Structure and Constituency of the Languages of the Americas* (2000 and 2003).